The End of the World

Published in 2025 by Scientific American Educational Publishing
in association with **The Rosen Publishing Group**
2544 Clinton Street, Buffalo NY 14224

Contains material from Scientific American®, a division of Springer Nature America, Inc.,
reprinted by permission, as well as original material from The Rosen Publishing Group®.

First Edition

Scientific American
Lisa Pallatroni: Project Editor

Rosen Publishing
Michael Hessel-Mial: Compiling Editor
Michael Moy: Senior Graphic Designer

Cataloging-in-Publication Data
Names: Scientific American, Inc.
Title: The end of the world / edited by the Scientific American Editors.
Description: First Edition. | New York : Scientific American Educational Publishing, 2025. |
Series: Scientific American explores big ideas | Includes bibliographical references and index.
Identifiers: ISBN 9781725351653 (pbk.) | ISBN 9781725351660
(library bound) | ISBN 9781725351677 (ebook)
Subjects: LCSH: End of the world (Astronomy). | Extinction (Biology)–Juvenile literature.
Classification: LCC QB638.8 E53 2025 | DDC 001.9–dc23

Manufactured in the United States of America
Websites listed were live at the time of publication.

Cover: Vadim Sadovski/Shutterstock.com

CPSIA Compliance Information: Batch # CSSA25.
For Further Information contact Rosen Publishing at 1-800-237-9932.

CONTENTS

INTRODUCTION

Ever since 18th-century scientist Georges Cuvier proved that species could go extinct, humans have pondered the science of their own demise. Later insights, like the discovery of the dinosaur-killing asteroid or the inevitable heat death of the universe, have brought home the difficult truth that we will not exist forever. Given contemporary threats like pandemics, climate change, and nuclear war, science can help us better understand our likelihood of doom, and help us survive. The articles in this title explore many such scenarios.

The opening section reminds us that we respond to cataclysm in a human way, especially highlighting how disasters impact us psychologically. The second section, on previous mass extinctions, reveals parallels to the present. Environmental shifts like climate change played a significant role in past die-offs. The third section on pandemics surveys threats that might surpass the death toll of COVID-19. Though pandemics seem less likely to permanently defeat us, the rapid evolution of diseases still threatens the lives of millions. The fourth section covers the risk of asteroid collisions; aerospace and defense agencies have spent millions preparing possible ways to fend off a colliding asteroid. The fifth section explores the most significant threat of our age: climate change. Thousands of species, including our own, are vulnerable to this danger that we have so far failed to prevent. The sixth section explores another human-made danger: nuclear war. The scientific consensus has concluded that there is no safe exchange of nuclear strikes. The final section explores the most remote and most inevitable doom: the death of our sun and eventual heat death of the universe. Billions of years into the future, this truth throws our fragility into relief.

Though these articles are a sharp reminder of some serious dangers, what the science does not require us to do is fall into hopelessness. Humans cannot avoid death, but they can choose to care for one another and plan for the risks of the future. In a way, the careful study of these risks can help cultivate a wiser kind of optimism.

Section 1: Introducing Disaster

How the Stress of Disaster Brings People Together

By Emma Seppala

E ver feel that stress makes you more cranky, hot-headed, or irritable? For men in particular, we think of stress as generating testosterone-fueled aggression—thus instances of road rage, or the need to "blow off steam" after work with a trip to the gym or a bar. On the other hand, in circumstances of extreme stress such as during natural disasters like Hurricane Sandy, we hear moving accounts of people going out of their way to help others. Hurricane Sandy has led to a flourish of supportive tweets and Facebook messages directed to people on the East Coast. The tsunami in Asia a couple of years ago led to a huge influx of financial support to help afflicted areas. Many who lived in New York City during 9/11 remember that, for a few days afterward, the boundaries and class divisions between people dissolved: people greeted each other on the street and were more considerate, sensitive to each other, and gentle than normal.

The classic view is that, under stress, men respond with "fight or flight," i.e. they become aggressive or leave the scene, whereas women are more prone to "tend and befriend," as has been shown in research by Shelley Taylor. A new study by Markus Heinrichs and Bernadette von Dawans at the University of Freiburg, Germany, however, suggests that acute stress may actually lead to greater cooperative, social, and friendly behavior, even in men. This more positive and social response could help explain the human connection that happens during times of crises, a connection that may be responsible, at least in part, for our collective survival as a species.

In Heinrichs' and Dawans' study, male participants were assigned to either an experimental group, with a stress procedure (a public speaking exercise followed by a complicated mental arithmetics), or a control group with no stress. They all were then asked to play an economics game involving potential financial gain based on the choices they make. In this game, they could choose to cooperate with others and trust them or not. The researchers found that, rather than becoming more aggressive after stress, men in the stress group actually became more trusting of others, displayed more trustworthy behavior themselves, and were more likely to cooperate and share profits. The researchers also found that these results were not due to weakened judgment in the stress group: the stress group did not differ from the control groups in their ability to make decisions or their willingness to sanction another participant who behaved unfairly.

One reason why stress may lead to cooperative behavior is our profound need for social connection. Human beings are fundamentally social animals and it is the protective nature of our social relationships that has allowed our species to thrive. Decades of research shows that social connection is a fundamental human need linked to both psychological and physical health including a stronger immune system, faster recovery from disease and even longevity.

Social connection may be particularly important under stress because stress naturally leads to a sense of vulnerability and loss of control. A study by Benjamin Converse and colleagues at the University of Virginia found that feeling out of control (through a reminder of one's mortality) leads to greater generosity and helpfulness while research at Stanford University by Aneeta Rattan and Krishna Savani showed that the opposite is true when we are primed with feelings of self-determination and control. Think back to a time when you felt out of control, for example during a romantic break-up, when you had an empty bank account, or after you lost a job. Chances are your feeling of vulnerability and feelings of lack of control may have made you seek the comfort of others in some way. Brene Brown, Professor at the University of Houston Graduate College of Social Work and expert in the field of social connection, explains that vulnerability is a core ingredient of social bonding.

War is one of the greatest stresses anyone could ever encounter yet it also often leads to deep human friendships and incredible acts of heroism and sacrifice for one other. In my research with returning veterans, I have often heard them speak of the tight bond that occurs between servicemembers on the battlefield—one of the most stressful situations that exists. Countless soldiers have perished running into a line of fire to save an injured brother-in-arms. Some believe that it is these experiences of profound human bonding that, despite the acute anguishes of war, makes some veterans long to return to war.

If stress leads to bonding, why then do we sometimes experience stress as making us cranky? The cause may be explained by a difference between acute and chronic stress. We know from research by Robert Sapolsky that acute stress prepares the body for resistance (physiological readiness, increased immune response, and heightened awareness) but that chronic stress slowly beats down the body. It may be that "acute" stress, i.e. a one-time stressful experience may lead to social bonding, as shown in the study, but that "chronic" stress, i.e. repeated exposure to stress over a long period, might wear us out. More research is needed to thoroughly examine the impact of chronic stress on social behavior.

Acute stress may help remind us of a fundamental truth: our common humanity. Understanding our shared vulnerability—life makes no promises—may be frightening, but it can inspire kindness, connection, and desire to stand together and support each other. Acute stress, as unpleasant as it may be, may also be an opportunity to experience the most beautiful aspects of life: social connection and love.

Psychology Reveals the Comforts of the Apocalypse

By Daisy Yuhas

D ecember 21, according to much-hyped misreadings of the Mayan calendar, will mark the end of the world. It's not the first "end is nigh" proclamation—and it's unlikely to be the last. That's because, deep down for various reasons, there's something appealing—at least to some of us—about the end of the world.

Enjoy the Self-Fulfilling Prophecy

University of Minnesota neuroscientist Shmuel Lissek, who studies the fear system, believes that at its heart, the concept of doomsday evokes an innate and ancient bias in most mammals. "The initial response to any hint of alarm is fear. This is the architecture with which we're built," Lissek says. Over evolutionary history, organisms with a better-safe-than-sorry approach survive. This mechanism has had consequences for both the body and brain, where the fast-acting amygdala can activate a fearful stress response before "higher" cortical areas have a chance to assess the situation and respond more rationally.

But why would anyone enjoy kindling this fearful response? Lissek suspects that some apocalyptic believers find the idea that the end is nigh to be validating. Individuals with a history of traumatic experiences, for example, may be fatalistic. For these people, finding a group of like-minded fatalists is reassuring. There may also be comfort in being able to attribute doom to some larger cosmic order—such as an ancient Mayan prophecy. This kind of mythology removes any sense of individual responsibility.

There's an even broader allure to knowing the precise end date. "Apocalyptic beliefs make existential threats—the fear of our mortality—predictable," Lissek says. Lissek, in collaboration with National Institute of Mental Health neuroscientist Christian Grillon and colleagues, has found that when an unpleasant or painful experience, such as an electric shock, is predictable, we relax. The anxiety produced by uncertainty is gone. Knowing when the end will come doesn't appeal equally to everyone, of course—but for many of us it's paradoxically a reason to stop worrying.

This also means people can focus on preparing. Doomsday preppers who assemble their bunker and canned food, Lissek believes, are engaged in goal-oriented behaviors, which are a proven therapy in times of trouble.

The Power of Knowledge

Beyond the universal aspects of fear and our survival response to it, certain personality traits may make individuals more susceptible to believing it's the end of the world. Social psychologist Karen Douglas at the University of Kent studies conspiracy theorists and suspects that her study subjects, in some cases, share attributes with those who believe in an impending apocalypse. She points out that, although these are essentially two different phenomena, certain apocalyptic beliefs are also at the heart of conspiracy theories—for example, the belief that government agencies know about an impending disaster and are intentionally hiding this fact to prevent panic.

"One trait I see linking the two is the feeling of powerlessness, often connected to a mistrust in authority," Douglas says. Among conspiracy theorists, these convictions of mistrust and impotence make their conspiracies more precious—and real. "People feel like they have knowledge that others do not."

Relatively few studies exist on the individuals who start and propagate these theories. Douglas points out that research into the psychology of persuasion has found that those who believe most are also most motivated to broadcast their beliefs. In the internet age, that's an easier feat than ever before.

Lessons from Dystopia

Steven Schlozman, drawing both from his experiences as a Harvard Medical School child psychiatrist and novelist (his first book recounts a zombie apocalypse) believes it's the post-apocalyptic landscape that fascinates people most.

"I talk to kids in my practice and they see it as a good thing. They say, 'life would be so simple—I'd shoot some zombies and wouldn't have to go to school,'" Schlozman says. In both literature and in speaking with patients, Schlozman has noticed that people frequently romanticize the end times. They imagine surviving, thriving, and going back to nature.

Schlozman recently had an experience that eerily echoed Orson Welles's 1938 *The War of the Worlds* broadcast. He was discussing his book on a radio program and they had to cut the show short when listeners misconstrued his fiction for fact. He believes the propensity to panic is not constant in history but instead reflects the times. In today's complicated world with terrorism, war, fiscal cliffs, and climate change, people are primed for panic.

"All of this uncertainty and all of this fear comes together and people think maybe life would be better" after a disaster, Schlozman says. Of course, in truth, most of their post-apocalyptic dreams are just fantasies that ignore the real hardships of pioneer life and crumbling infrastructure. He points out that, if anything, tales of apocalypse, particularly involving zombies, should ideally teach us something about the world we should avoid—and how to make necessary changes now.

This article was published in Scientific American's former blog network and reflects the views of the author, not necessarily those of Scientific American

About the Author

Daisy Yuhas edits the Scientific American *column Mind Matters. She is a freelance science journalist and editor based in Austin, Tex. Follow Yuhas on X (formerly Twitter) @DaisyYuhas*

Fix Disaster Response Now

By the Editors of *Scientific American*

G iven record-breaking wildfires, hurricanes, and other weather disasters that cost lives and billions of dollars amid a pandemic that brought death to every corner of the country, the events of 2020 stretched U.S. emergency management institutions. Local governments have been unable to cope with the disasters, and the Federal Emergency Management Agency (FEMA) has been strained. This litany of destruction has brought into stark relief problems of capacity and inequity—people of color and low-income communities have been hit disproportionately hard—that have been festering for decades in the nation's approach to disaster preparedness. Now, with the climate crisis increasing the odds of calamities, we must stop kicking the can down the road and commit to the challenging work of revamping emergency management.

FEMA is supposed to be the agency that steps in when disasters overwhelm local resources, whereas cities, counties, and states handle smaller events. But a FEMA National Advisory Council (NAC) report last November noted that state and local emergency management operations struggle even with routine events. Some towns and counties have only a part-time emergency manager, leaving them ill-equipped to prepare for and respond to disasters. As a result, they increasingly turn to FEMA, which ends up with fewer resources to spare when a major catastrophe does occur. When Hurricane Harvey flooded southeastern Texas in 2017 with an unprecedented 60 inches of rain, for example, almost half of the agency's emergency workforce had already been deployed to other trouble spots. To free itself up, FEMA is now proposing to raise the damage threshold that triggers federal assistance. But that proposal simply will leave local areas more vulnerable. Congress or state legislatures need to supply sustainable funds that build and maintain local emergency management departments, along with any change in the rules for FEMA involvement.

To address the problem that all emergency agencies do little in advance to prepare for disasters, some funding could be earmarked for—and require—certain crucial mitigation work sometimes resisted by local political forces, such as elevating structures in flood-prone areas or instituting zoning laws to reduce wildfire risks. These efforts should incorporate the latest climate science—sea-level-rise projections, for example—so they do not quickly become obsolete. The National Institute of Building Sciences has found that for every $1 that FEMA and other federal agencies spend on mitigating the risks of floods, earthquakes, and other hazards, society ultimately saves $6 in costs.

Any future mitigation and recovery funding must also be distributed in an equitable way. Research, including a 2019 study published in *Social Problems*, has shown that FEMA programs inadvertently entrench and exacerbate inequities because they focus on restoring private property. This approach favors higher-income, typically majority white areas with more valuable homes and infrastructure over people of color and low-income communities, which are both disproportionately affected by disaster and least able to recover from it. To remedy this disparity, FEMA, as well as state and local emergency management agencies, cannot rely solely on cost-benefit analyses to determine what projects to fund, because these weigh in favor of more expensive properties. They should also use other metrics, such as the Social Vulnerability Index, which identifies the populations with the least capacity to deal with disasters. Some local governments have begun to incorporate equity into their emergency planning. In Washington State's King County, for example, floodplain managers have used census data to understand exactly who lives in flood-prone areas to better target resources and mitigation projects. Others should follow their lead.

One current FEMA program has tried to tackle inequity issues by allowing small, low-income communities to pay less in cost matching, which is a precondition of some FEMA aid. But these smaller governments may not have dedicated staff with the expertise to navigate the complex FEMA application process. In some cases, communities may not have the funds to meet even a lowered threshold for local spending. FEMA can begin to solve this by simplifying its funding requirements and instituting a single application process; both actions were recommended by the NAC report and in February by the Government Accountability Office.

Everyone, not just the well-to-do, should have the opportunity to build back their lives with the resources they need in the wake of disaster.

Will Humans Ever Go Extinct?

The species *Homo sapiens* evolved some 300,000 years ago and has come to dominate Earth unlike any species that came before. But how long can humans last?

Eventually humans will go extinct. According to the most wildly optimistic estimate, our species will last perhaps another billion years but end when the expanding envelope of the sun swells outward and heats the planet to a Venus-like state.

But a billion years is a long time. One billion years ago life on Earth consisted of microbes. Multicellular life didn't make its debut until about 600 million years ago, when sponges proliferated. What life will look like in another billion years is anyone's guess, but one modeling study published in 2021 in *Nature Geoscience* suggests that Earth's atmosphere will contain very little oxygen by then, meaning that anaerobic microbes, rather than humans, will probably be the last living Earthlings.

If surviving to see the sun fry Earth is a long shot, when is humanity likely to meet its doom? Paleontologically, mammalian species usually persist for about a million years, says Henry Gee, a paleontologist and senior editor at the journal *Nature*, whose forthcoming book is on the extinction of humans. That would put the human species in its youth. But Gee doesn't think these rules necessarily apply for *H. sapiens*.

"Humans are rather an exceptional species," he says. "We could last for millions of years, or we could all drop down next week."

Opportunities for doomsday abound. Humans could be wiped out by a catastrophic asteroid strike, commit self-destruction with worldwide nuclear war, or succumb to the ravages caused by the climate emergency. But humans are a hardy bunch, so the most likely scenario involves a combination of catastrophes that could eradicate us completely.

Pick Your Poison

Some species killers are out of our control. In a 2021 paper in the journal *Icarus*, for example, researchers describe how asteroids comparable to the one spanning 10 to 15 kilometers in diameter that killed off the nonavian dinosaurs hit Earth approximately every 250 million to 500 million years. In a preprint paper posted on the server arXiv.org, physicists Philip Lubin and Alexander N. Cohen calculate that humanity would have the ability to save itself from a dino-killer-size asteroid, given six months' warning and an arsenal of nuclear penetrators to blow the space rock into a cloud of harmless pebbles. With less warning or a larger asteroid, Lubin and Cohen suggest, humanity should give up and "party" or "move to Mars or the moon to party." Currently the biggest asteroid that scientists know of with the potential to strike Earth is called (29075) 1950 DA. It is a mere 1,300 meters across and has a one-in-50,000 chance of hitting our world in March 2880, according to a 2022 risk analysis by the European Space Agency.

Incoming space rocks aside, many threats to humanity are of our own making: nuclear war, the climate emergency, ecological collapse. We might be done in by our own tech in the form of sentient artificial intelligence that decides to snuff out its creators, as some AI critics have suggested.

An all-out nuclear war could easily destroy humanity, says François Diaz-Maurin, associate editor for nuclear affairs at the *Bulletin of the Atomic Scientists*. The last time humans dropped nuclear bombs on one another, only one country, the U.S., had nuclear warheads, so there was no risk of nuclear retaliation. That's not the case today—and now the bombs are a lot bigger. Those older bombs, which struck the Japanese cities of Hiroshima and Nagasaki in 1945, packed the equivalent of 15 and 21 kilotons of TNT, respectively. Together they killed an estimated 110,000 to 210,000 people. A single modern-day, 300-kiloton nuclear weapon dropped on New York City, for example, would kill a million people in 24 hours, Diaz-Maurin says. A regional nuclear war, such as one between India and Pakistan, could kill 27 million people in the short term, whereas a full-scale nuclear war between the U.S. and Russia could cause an estimated 360 million direct deaths, he adds.

The threat to humanity's very existence would come after the war, when soot from massive fires ignited by the bombings would rapidly alter the climate in a scenario known as nuclear winter. Fears of nuclear winter may have receded since the end of the cold war, Diaz-Maurin says, but research shows that the environmental consequences would be severe. Even a regional nuclear war would damage the ozone layer, block out sunlight, and reduce precipitation worldwide. The result would be a global famine that might kill more than five billion people in just two years, depending on the size and number of detonations.

"That possibility of destroying humanity is still here and real," Diaz-Maurin says.

Death by ecological contamination or the climate emergency would be slower but still within the realm of possibility. Already humans are facing health stressors from chronic pollution that have been exacerbated by the additional heat brought on by climate change, says Maureen Lichtveld, dean of the School of Public Health at the University of Pittsburgh. Hotter temperatures force people to breathe more rapidly to dispel warmth, which draws more pollution into their lungs. The climate emergency also deepens existing problems around food security—for instance, persistent drought can devastate cropland—and infectious disease. "The interconnectedness of climate change and health inequities and inequities in general is what is impacting our global population," Lichtveld says.

The Perfect Storm

Will these inequities eventually lead to a species-wide downfall? It's not easy to calculate the likelihood that, say, the climate emergency will kill us all, says Luke Kemp, a research affiliate at the Center for the Study of Existential Risk at the University of Cambridge. But it's probably not realistic to consider risks individually anyway, he says.

"When we look at the history of things like mass extinctions and societal collapses, it's never just one thing that happens," Kemp says. "If you're trying to rely on a single silver bullet to kill everyone in a single event, you have to write sci-fi."

The end of humanity is far more likely to be brought about by multiple factors, Kemp says—a pileup of disasters. Although apocalyptic movies often turn to viruses, bacteria, and fungi to wipe out huge swathes of the population, a pandemic alone probably won't drive humanity to extinction simply because the immune system is a broad and effective defense, says Amesh Adalja, an infectious disease physician and senior scholar at the Johns Hopkins Center for Health Security. A pandemic could be devastating and lead to severe upheaval—the Black Death killed 30 to 50 percent of Europe's population—but it's unlikely that a pathogen would kill all of humanity, Adalja says. "Yes, an infectious disease could kill a lot of people," he says, "but then you're going to have a group [of people] that are resilient to it and survive."

Humans also have tools to fight back against a pathogen, from medical treatments to vaccines to the social-distancing measures that became familiar worldwide during the COVID pandemic, Adalja says. There is one example of a mammalian species that may have been entirely eliminated by an infectious disease, he says: the Christmas Island rat (*Rattus macleari*), also called Maclear's rat, an endemic island species that may have gone extinct because of the introduction of a parasite.

"We are not helpless like the Christmas Island rat, which couldn't get away from that island," Adalja says. "We have the ability to change our fate."

If infectious disease contributes to the downfall of humanity, it will probably be as just one piece of a larger puzzle. Imagine a planet pushed to upheaval by sea-level rise and disruption to agriculture from climate change. The humans of this climate-ravaged world attempt a geoengineering solution that goes wrong. The situation worsens. Resources are scarce, and a bunch of countries have nuclear weapons. Oh, by the way, the mosquitoes that carry yellow fever range as far north as Canada in this scenario. It's not hard to see how the human population could decline and disappear in the face of an arsenal of challenges, according to Kemp.

Worst-case scenarios are understudied, Kemp says. In climate science, for example, there is a lot of research into what the world might look like at two or three degrees Celsius warmer than the preindustrial average but very little looking at what an increase of five or six degrees C might look like. This is partly because scientists have a hard time predicting the effects of that much warming and partly because climate scientists feel pressure from politicians not to appear alarmist, Kemp says. Models of future worst-case scenarios also tend to do an inadequate job of predicting the cascading effects of a disaster. "The general field of existential risk is relatively new, nascent, and just understudied," Kemp says.

There are questions as to how much humans should worry about something as big picture as extinction. While some see the question as pressing—controversial tech billionaires such as Elon Musk and Peter Thiel have funded organizations dedicated to studying the risks of transformative technologies—others argue that today's problems are urgent enough. Already humans are heating the globe, overexploiting and destroying nature, using land and water unsustainably, and creating chemicals that are harmful to all life, often in service to the globally well-off, says Sarah Cornell, who studies global sustainability at the Stockholm Resilience Center at Stockholm University.

"Today's reality is that some human beings are undermining or even destroying living conditions of many, many other people," Cornell says. "From a human-scale perspective, this is an existential crisis already, not a risk somewhere up ahead."

About the Author

Stephanie Pappas is a freelance science journalist. She is based in Denver, Colo.

Section 2: Ancient Apocalypses

What Ancient Mass Extinctions Tell Us about the Future

By Peter Brannen

Pangaea, 252 million years ago—the world is over. Siberia has been erupting for 300,000 years, is still erupting, and won't stop. Not a volcano, mind you, but Siberia—two million square miles of it. A suppurating, billowing, continent-scaled wasteland of glowing rock and steam. The seas, once resplendent with horn corals and sponge reefs, are now sour and laden with mercury. Hot as soup, they bubble deathly swamp gas that feeds vile, hurricane-churned slicks of slime. The seabed is vacant, as scuttling trilobites die out after a quarter of a billion years. Beside this rancid ocean, on the shores of a blasted supercontinent, the forests are gone. Instead hot rivers now spill over the dead land in wide braids. Fungus blooms where vanished groves of ferns once held contests full of fangs and armor—gorgonopsids battling pareiasaurs. Their final bones are now scoured by hot winds and bleached by a searing sunlight, unfiltered by ozone. Night falls and brings odd constellations that light the dead waves, lapping at dead shores, tossing old bits of a dead reef from a dead sea. It smells awful. The planet is ruin and slime and heat. The ocean suffocates. Bacterial mounds spread. A hundred thousand suns rise and fall on a hopeless world. A hundred thousand springtimes arrive with no respite. It's still all but barren. A million years of misery pass. Ten million.

At long last, the planet is finally reborn—this time with dinosaurs and ichthyosaurs and pterosaurs and mammals and turtles and sturgeon—almost as if a new story entirely has begun, exuberant, confident, vital: the Mesozoic era. The old story, too dark to retell, has long been filed away somewhere deep in the great cabinets of Earth, along with an epitaph in the rocks, written in geochemistry: carbon dioxide destroyed this world.

Mass extinctions are not merely bad days in Earth history. They are not even very bad days. They are the very, very worst days in the entire half-billion-year history of complex life. They are supremely horrifying, astronomically rare, global Ragnaroks that end the lineages of most living creatures on the planet. They are terrible, surreal things: 20,000 years of suffocating greenhouse heat punctuated by volcanic winter blasts or an afternoon of celestial terror and tsunamis. And until around 1980, they were mostly thought to be disreputable speculation.

Over the past two centuries the field of geology, like the fossil record itself, has been characterized by long periods of stasis punctuated by exhilarating moments of upheaval and innovation. It would be arbitrary to identify *one* founding figure for the modern study of geology, but one could do worse than Scottish geologist James Hutton, who did much to reveal the "abyss of time" underneath us. At a salt-sprayed Siccar Point on the eastern coast of Scotland in 1788, he spied an outcrop made of two kinds of rock, one stacked on top of the other, meeting abruptly in the middle. But the rock on the bottom—laminations of deep-sea muck—had been formed at the bottom of the ocean, tilted sideways, thrust up into the air and planed off by wind and erosion. And the rock on the top had been formed by tropical rivers on dry land. The missing time implied between the two rocks, now conjoined but separated by an unthinkable gap, shattered Hutton. The body of his writing is notoriously obtuse and unimpressive; he apparently saved all his eloquence for one haunting observation that, in the confusion of Earth beneath our feet, "we find no vestige of a beginning, no prospect of an end." Although the history of humanity has played out in the shallows so far, time, it turns out, is *deep*.

Geologists cast off the strictures of biblical time and Noah's flood, and their new field matured over the decades, spurred by a significant material reward for finding coal and minerals in a strange new industrial age. The story of life on Earth, however fragmentary and tantalizing, slowly revealed itself.

At this magazine's founding in the mid-1800s, the field was in its adolescence. It was still dominated by men of means—the kind of ascotted dilettantes rendered humorlessly in oil and lithograph portraits. The contributions of women such as Mary Anning, the unmatched fossil hunter who scoured the English shoreline unearthing the local "snakestones" and "stone crocodiles" that littered the wave-battered Jurassic Coast, were acknowledged only sheepishly. Although *Scientific American* headlines from the time still hint at a somewhat rudimentary state of affairs ("Experts Doubt the Sun Is Actually Burning Coal"), by midcentury geology had nonetheless been established as an empirical, systematized field of inquiry with roots in antiquity—one of the many such intellectual eddies that swirled out of Enlightenment-era "natural philosophy." That is, it now had rules. The rules were deceptively simple and powerful. Layers of ocean rock now propped up at unusual angles on land must have once laid flat on a seafloor in some distant age. Dikes of old magma that pierced this stony tiramisu must have worked their shoots into the layered rock sometime after. The fossils entombed in these rock layers could be correlated to those fossils and those rocks with the same layers, way over there.

In 1860 English geologist John Phillips drew on the fossil-collecting labor of decades prior, and a growing body of paleontology literature scattered across elegant monographs, to plot a surprisingly modern curve of the richness of life over Earth history, the first ever such diagram. The graph ominously included two profound dips in life: one crash that separated the trilobite-spangled Paleozoic era from the dinosaur-haunted Mesozoic era and another plunge that separated the Mesozoic from our own Cenozoic time (all terms of Phillips's invention). The dramatic breaks in fossil life hinted at some kind of ancient calamity that divided the great ages and supported the blasphemous idea that species—that is, God's very Creation— might go extinct, which had been proposed half a century earlier by the renowned French naturalist Georges Cuvier. On considering the odd elephant bones that littered the New World, of mammoths and mastodons (*"animal de l'Ohio"*), Cuvier had proposed that life on Earth, like French rule, could be swept away in "revolutions." Phillips's graph provided something close to quantitative proof, and Phillips himself thought that each recovery consisted of separate acts of divine creation. Yet it would take more than a century for anyone to take the idea of mass extinctions seriously again.

This is because, by the end of the 19th century, the field was still dominated, and would continue to be dominated for decades, by the enduring framework of "uniformitarianism." This concept, popularized by Charles Lyell, is summarized in a catchphrase still taught to geology students: "The present is the key to the past." That is, the unhurried processes at work on the face of Earth today—the relentless if unimpressive work of rain on rock, the inexorable incision of rivers into highlands, or the piling of sand into desert dunes—have always been plying the planet in the same tedious fashion and could account for everything we find in the rock record. Painting on this vast new canvas of time, Charles Darwin would propose that similarly small but steady biological changes over generations, filtered by the relentless tournament of life and death, and given Hutton's eons to ramify, could produce the "endless forms" of life "most beautiful" on Earth today. Pointedly absent from this measured account of planetary history were the gauche cataclysms of Cuvier and Phillips.

Geology was upended in the middle of the 20th century by the plate tectonic revolution—the validation of the once fringe idea that continents drifted across the world like rudderless ships. Even so, the idea of sudden apocalyptic global mass extinctions remained suspect at best. Catastrophism was spooky, reminiscent of a benighted prescientific world where capricious gods subjected the world to cleansing acts of global destruction. Worse, speculation about why the dinosaurs had disappeared had become something of a cottage industry among cranks, and serious scientists were nervous about associating with a crowd who proposed, among dozens of other incoherent ideas for their demise, "dwindling brain and consequent stupidity," development of heads that became "too heavy to lift," "psychotic suicidal factors," "competition with caterpillars," "terminal hay fever," and "methane poisoning from dinosaur flatulence." And yet the orthodoxy began to crack.

"*Neokatastrophismus?*" the iconoclastic German scientist Otto Schindewolf asked of his fellow paleontologists in 1963, attempting to revive Cuvier's catastrophism for the 20th century. Because his question was posed in German, few English-speaking scientists felt the need to reply. But Schindewolf could no longer overlook the ominous interruption of life he saw—among other places—exposed in the ancient rocks of the Salt Range in Pakistan. There appeared to be a dreadful global collapse of the ocean ecosystem at the end of the Permian period a quarter of a billion years ago (in fact, the greatest mass extinction in Earth history), just as Phillips had plotted more than a century prior. Schindewolf conscripted a supernova for his vision of the apocalypse, proposing that it might have irradiated Earth and seeded the biosphere with ruinous mutations.

In that same year, American Norman Newell, plotting the fates of 2,500 animal families over Earth history, noted six intervals when extinction seemed to cut a broad swath through all of life, instead proposing dramatic sea-level changes as his preferred Grim Reaper. And at the end of the decade Digby McLaren, director of the Canadian Geological Survey's Institute of Sedimentary and Petroleum Geology, insisted in his 1969 presidential address to the Paleontological Society that his fellow paleontologists were trying to "define out of existence" the obvious breaks in the fossil record, such as a devastating wave of death 375 million years ago that wiped out the largest global reef system in the history of life. "I cannot accept a uniformitarian explanation," he said of the catastrophe, glaringly apparent in ancient rocks from Iran to Alberta. McLaren had an idea for what could cause such a discontinuity.

"I shall, therefore, land a large or very large meteorite in the Paleozoic Pacific," he announced, capable of generating "a wave 20 thousand feet high. This will do." McLaren's address, it is reported, was "met with embarrassed silence," and many paleontologists in the audience, still under Lyell's spell, assumed he must have been joking.

Then, in 1980, an asteroid landed in the field. Walter Alvarez, then a young University of California, Berkeley, professor, was traipsing the Apennines above the medieval Italian town of Gubbio. In this mountainous pile of ancient limestone seafloor, pushed up by the grinding advance of Africa into Europe, there was a sharp break—a lifeless clay layer—between the placid sea life of dinosaur times and the impoverished life of the early age of mammals. Perhaps this transformative interval took place over millions of years, validating the uniformitarian view. Or perhaps Cuvier and Phillips had it right all along, and the turnover was devastatingly short. Curious, Alvarez recruited his father, Luis, a Nobel-winning physicist, to help tackle the question. It was quite the second act for the elder Alvarez, a pioneer of military radar technology and Manhattan Project alum who helped to develop the atomic bomb and even watched "Little Boy" explode over Hiroshima from an attending B-29. His wartime work became unexpectedly relevant to the catastrophe they were investigating, which throttled the planet some 66 million years earlier.

The Alvarezes knew that unusual elements like iridium were delivered to Earth from above by an eternal drizzle of space dust, at a steady rate. Measure the iridium in the ominous clay layer, they reasoned, and if there's just a little bit, the dramatic turnover in life couldn't have taken very long. Conversely, if there's a lot of iridium, it took a very long time indeed. But what if, as they discovered, there was 100 times more iridium than they ever expected? After bombarding the clay samples with neutrons from a nuclear reactor and analyzing them, the Alvarezes were astonished. The only vehicle large enough for this much exotic material was not a light drizzle of space dust but one truly gigantic space rock. (Often omitted in this account, though not by the Alvarezes themselves, is the fact that Dutch geologist Jan Smit and Belgian geologist Jan Hertogen made the very same discovery among ancient ocean rocks in Spain at the very same time and even published their results in the journal *Nature* two weeks earlier than the Alvarezes' landmark *Science* paper.)

28

The resulting chaos from such an impact would be like all-out nuclear warfare, only worse. There would be the unimaginable heat from the initial explosion, which would have been thousands of times more powerful than the detonation of all the nuclear weapons on Earth at the height of the cold war, all in one place, all at once. "Certainly enough," as one impact modeler put it to me, "to lift a mountain back into space at escape velocity." It has been proposed that as this spacebound ejecta encircled the globe, it might have turned the atmosphere into a pizza oven for 20 minutes (with dinosaurs playing the role of pepperoni). Then there might have been the decades of darkness and cold from the nuclear winter to follow, starving any lingering creature lucky enough to have avoided being evaporated outright by the asteroid, swept up in its tsunamis, or turned to charcoal by the ballistic reentry of its debris into the atmosphere.

In 1991 whatever lingering skepticism about the impact that remained among uniformitarian hardliners was wiped away by the discovery of a 110-mile crater buried under tens of millions of years of limestone on Mexico's Yucatán peninsula. In fact, the crater had already been discovered in 1978 by geophysicists working for the Mexican national oil company Pemex, but they had announced their findings at a geophysics conference that had escaped notice of paleontologists for more than a decade. And the structure had been found some 1,000 years earlier by the Maya, who built settlements around limestone sinkholes that pock the Yucatán and that provided freshwater. The pattern of these sinkholes reflects the deeply disturbed rock far below and maps almost exactly onto the crater's edge, in a 110-mile ring.

Popular culture took note. The 1990s saw a rash of impact-inspired cable specials and movies strewn with bad CGI, which—along with the astounding, apocalypse-scaled collision of Comet Shoemaker-Levy 9 with Jupiter in 1994—were sufficient to convince the public of the dangers of space rocks. This is typically where the story ends. As far as most people are concerned, mass extinctions are what happen when big things fall out of the sky.

But something funny happened over the next 30 years as geologists fanned out across the globe to look for convincing evidence of impacts—such as layers of iridium, shocked quartz or giant craters—at the ominous rock boundaries that mark the four other major mass extinctions in Earth history. They didn't find any. And all but one of the so-called Big Five mass extinctions were *even more severe* than the catastrophe that wiped out the nonbird dinosaurs.

In fact, there even existed major impact structures, such as the Triassic-age 62-mile-wide Manicouagan Crater in Quebec (now a circular system of lakes amid a boreal paradise of blackflies) or the massive crater that created the Chesapeake Bay 36 million years ago, that did not seem to bother life much at all. Given the remarkable correlation of the Yucatán impact with the disappearance of the large dinosaurs (and much of the rest of life on Earth at the end of the Cretaceous period), this came as a surprise. Stranger still, the stunning finale of the age of dinosaurs was also accompanied not only by an envoy from outer space but by one of the largest volcanic events in the history of animal life: a swath of eruptions that drowned much of India *miles* deep in lava. While the consensus is that the asteroid did most of the damage, this was the same class of world-changing eruptions responsible not only for dozens of minor mass extinctions and climate misadventures throughout Earth history but several of the other major mass extinctions as well, including the worst ever at the end of the Permian 252 million years ago.

In the past few decades a subtler story about mass extinctions has emerged. Geologists are now armed with powerful techniques Hutton couldn't have dreamed of. Scattering to remote rock outcrops around the world or to archives of muck hoisted from the bottom of the ocean by drill ships, they wring secrets out of old seashells with mass spectrometers, and from age-battered hunks of granite with radioisotope geochronology, and from fossil and geochemical databases with neural networks underwritten by blistering processing power. And in this diffuse project to understand Earth history, geologists have in recent years revealed a roster of existential threats to life far more intimate than simply death from above. The most frequent mass killer of life on Earth, it turns out, is Earth itself. And the most reliable murder weapon is carbon dioxide.

One hundred and thirty-five million years before a mindless hunk of space garbage intercepted Earth's orbit and ruined a perfectly good dinosaur world, the planet was gripped by a mass extinction that was even worse. A world of bizarre crocodilians, giant amphibians, stony corals, a ubiquity of strange but venerable eel-like creatures, and 80 percent of the rest of complex life on Earth was destroyed. As the supercontinent Pangaea pulled apart at the seams, stretching like taffy, an open sore of oozing, incandescent rock erupted at the surface, covering three million square miles in lava in pulses over 600,000 years. While the eruptions would have caused all sorts of chaos, perhaps most important they injected thousands of gigatons of carbon dioxide into the atmosphere, and the oceans overdosed on this volcanic CO_2. The seawater acidified as a simple matter of chemistry, and the temperature of the planet soared as a simple matter of physics. This is what CO_2 does. Today the New Jersey Palisades across the Hudson River from New York City are the volcanic plumbing that remains from these titanic eruptions of the Triassic end times, old magma that is matched by the same volcanic rock, of the same age, as far afield as Morocco, Brazil, Nova Scotia, and Spain.

Hundreds of millions of years earlier the two oldest major mass extinctions destroyed planets we wouldn't recognize, their continents misshapen and scattered about unfamiliar oceans. The oceans of these alien planets were patrolled by gigantic cephalopods and, later, even more gigantic fish, guillotine-mawed and fortified by helmets of bone. Our planet endlessly cycles carbon—the stuff of life—through rocks, air, water, and life in a balance that keeps the climate habitable and ocean chemistry hospitable. But these archaic worlds saw this carbon cycle suddenly derailed—unraveled by CO_2-sucking episodes of tropical mountain building, accelerated rock weathering, and the novel global geoengineering project of land plants. These kill mechanisms are somewhat more convoluted, and admittedly less dramatic, than an asteroid, but they did the trick. These bygone planets spun out of control, alternately freezing and broiling as Earth struggled to regain its composure and wrangle a global carbon cycle gone haywire.

But it was 252 million years ago, on the forsaken planet that opened this tour of ancient apocalypses—that sun-bleached world, with oceans almost absent of animals—when the story of life on Earth nearly came to its premature conclusion. This was Pangaea, a world before dinosaurs or mammals or flowers. But it was still a rich world, one with conifers and lithe, vaguely leonine predators and lumbering, warty, reptile prey. And then, it was over. It ended in a continent-scaled flood of glowing rock, brief volcanic winters issuing from the eruptions, and a roster of billowing volcanic gases, many of which would be banned on a battlefield—such as chlorine gas and mercury.

As the magma incinerated underground seams of salt and gypsum, eruptions of halocarbons would have obliterated the ozone layer—and indeed, plant fossils bear the mutations wrought by this ancient atmospheric destruction. But it wasn't until the seams of magma feeding these eruptions hit huge deposits of natural gas, coal, and carbon-rich rocks underground that the greatest mass extinction ever hit its appalling crescendo. Methane and carbon dioxide exploded out of the ground by the tens of thousands of gigatons. Temperatures spiked by almost 22 degrees Fahrenheit. And in the oceans, where spreading anoxia and acidification wiped out 96 percent of life, it was as hot as a jacuzzi. And then, in the fossil record, silence.

At the start of the industrial revolution, long slumbering forests of carbon were resurrected from the ancient Earth and pressed into service in the furnaces of modernity. We know that this artificial fire can't go on forever without immiserating our world. At 416 parts per million, carbon dioxide is already higher than it has been in millions of years and is perhaps rising even faster than in these greatest calamities of all time. Meanwhile centuries—millennia even—of hunting, land clearing, and pollution have impoverished the natural world. By one estimate, at the rate at which we are currently driving species extinct, we could match the biological devastation of those towering mass extinctions of the ancient past within 300 to 12,000 years. This might sound like a long time frame, but from a geologic perspective, it is downright subliminal. More worryingly, there may yet exist unseen ecological cliff edges along the way, beyond which the biosphere does not simply suffer the onslaught of attrition but collapses suddenly in cascading failures. In other words, there may be tipping points—points of no return.

We know what we have to do to avoid being inducted into the wretched pantheon of the worst things that have ever happened in Earth history. We must set aside swaths of the planet—in the form of marine protected areas, natural reserves, and corridors for migration—to allow the living world to recover from the uppercut we have already delivered it. Then, we must simply stop digging up old life from deep in Earth's crust and lighting it on fire at the surface. As humanity leans on the very same levers pulled in the very worst things that have ever happened in history, we must consult the ages and listen to the counsel of broken worlds past.

About the Author

Peter Brannen is a science journalist whose book The Ends of the World *is about the five major mass extinctions (Ecco, 2017). Brannen was a 2018–2019 Scripps Fellow at the University of Colorado Boulder.*

Dinosaur Asteroid Hit Worst-Case Place

By Julia Rosen

W e all know the story: 66 million years ago, a giant asteroid crashed into Earth, killing off three quarters of all species, including most of the dinosaurs. Researchers suspect that the impact caused the extinction by kicking up a cloud of dust and tiny droplets called aerosols that plunged the planet into something like a nuclear winter.

> "These components in the atmosphere drove global cooling and darkness that would have stopped photosynthesis from occurring, ultimately shutting down the food chain."
>
> Shelby Lyons, a recent Ph.D. graduate from Penn State University.

But scientists have also found lots of soot in the geologic layers deposited immediately after the asteroid impact. And the soot may have been part of the killing mechanism too—depending on where it came from.

Some of the soot probably came from wildfires that erupted around the planet following the impact. But most of these particles would have lingered in the lower atmosphere for only a few weeks and wouldn't have had much of an effect on global climate.

But scientists hypothesize that soot may also have come from the very rocks that the asteroid pulverized when it struck. If those rocks contained significant amounts of organic matter—such as the remains of marine organisms—it would have burned up on impact, sending soot shooting up into the stratosphere. In that case, soot would have spread around the globe in a matter of hours and stayed there for years. And it would have radically altered Earth's climate.

So Lyons and her team set out to identify the source of the soot. They looked at chemicals known as polycyclic aromatic hydrocarbons, or PAHs, which are another by-product of combustion.

"You can find PAHs in meat or veggies that you grill. You can find them from the exhaust of a car. You can also find them in smoke and debris from the wildfires today out west."

PAHs are made up of fused rings of carbon atoms—think of chicken wire. To determine the origin of the soot, the researchers looked at the structure and chemistry of the PAHs buried along with it. Specifically, the researchers looked for groups of atoms that stick off the rings like spikes. PAHs generated from burning wood don't have many spikes, but PAHs from burning fossil carbon—like what would have been in the target rocks—have more.

Lyons and her team found that most of the PAHs deposited after the impact were spiky, which suggests that soot from the rocks hit by the asteroid played a major role in the mass extinction.

"There was more dust and more sulfate aerosols than soot, but soot is a stronger blocker of sunlight than either of those two. So a small amount of soot can drive large reductions in sunlight."

The findings are in the *Proceedings of the National Academy of Sciences*. [Shelby L. Lyons et al., Organic matter from the Chicxulub crater exacerbated the K–Pg impact winter]

The results suggest that the devastation of this very sooty asteroid impact may be due in part to a fluke of geography: the space rock smashed into the Gulf of Mexico, where the sediments were rich in organic matter. They still are: the region produces large amounts of oil today.

"Where it had occurred was likely one of the reasons that it led to a major mass extinction. It was kind of the perfect storm, or the perfect asteroid impact, I guess you could call it."

[The above text is a transcript of this podcast.]

About the Author

Julia Rosen is an independent journalist covering science and the environment from Portland, Ore. Follow her on X (formerly Twitter) @1juliarosen.

Toxic Slime Contributed to Earth's Worst Mass Extinction— And It's Making a Comeback

By Chris Mays, Vivi Vajda and Stephen McLoughlin

At sunrise on a summer day in Australia, about an hour's drive from Sydney, we clambered northward along the base of a cliff on a mission. We were searching for rocks that we hoped would contain clues to the darkest chapter in our planet's history.

Life on Earth has experienced some terrifyingly close calls in the past four billion years—cataclysmic events in which the species driven to extinction outnumbered the survivors. The worst crisis occurred 252 million years ago, at the end of the Permian Period. Conditions back then were the bleakest that animals ever faced. Wildfires and drought scoured the land; oceans became intolerably hot and suffocating.

Very few creatures could survive in this hellscape. Ultimately more than 70 percent of land species and upward of 80 percent of ocean species went extinct, leading some paleontologists to call this dismal episode the Great Dying.

This calamity has been etched in stone across the globe but perhaps nowhere as clearly as on the rocky coasts of eastern Australia. By midmorning we had found our target: an outcrop of coal within the cliff face. Sedimentologist Christopher Fielding of the University of Connecticut, one of our longtime colleagues, had recently identified these rocks as river and lake sediments deposited during the end-Permian event. Following his lead, we had come to sift through the sediments for fossil remains from the few survivors of the arch extinction.

From our vantage point on the outcrop, we could see our first hint of ancient devastation: the absence of coal beds in the towering sandstone cliffs above us. During our dawn scramble across the rocks, we had spotted numerous coal beds sandwiched between the sandstones and mudstones in the lower rock levels. These coals date to the late Permian (around 259 million to 252 million years ago). They represent the compacted remains of the swamp forests that existed across a vast belt of the southern supercontinent Gondwana. In contrast, the younger, overlying rocks that span the early part of the subsequent Triassic Period, some 252 million to 247 million years ago, are devoid of coal. In fact, not a single coal seam has been found in rocks of this vintage anywhere in the world. Instead these strata reflect the peaceful deposition of sand and mud by rivers and lakes, seemingly undisturbed by life.

Historically ignored because of its paucity of fossil fuels for humans to exploit, this so-called coal gap has recently emerged as a key to understanding the history of life on Earth. We now know it was a symptom of a sick world. At the end of the Permian, not only did terrestrial and marine ecosystems collapse, but so, too, did freshwater ones. Recent studies by our team have shown that as global temperatures surged at the close of the Permian, blooms of bacteria and algae choked rivers and lakes, rendering them largely uninhabitable. Our findings help to explain why the ensuing mass extinction was so devastating—and raise concerns about the future of biodiversity in our warming world.

Scorched Earth

As the sun rose higher in the sky, its heat beat down on us relentlessly. We managed to pack in a few productive hours of fossil and rock collection before the outcrop became unbearably hot. At that time, in the early summer of 2018, it seemed warmer than the previous field season. Maybe it really was warmer, or maybe it was just because we had recently arrived from chilly Stockholm, where we work at the Swedish Museum of Natural History. Regardless, by midmorning we retreated to the shade for a couple of hours to cool down and ponder what we had seen.

We found the coals to consist almost entirely of compacted leaves, roots, and wood belonging to trees in the genus *Glossopteris*. *Glossopteris* trees flourished in wetlands and readily formed peat, a precursor to coal. Directly above the coals we saw no fossils at first. All the outcrops of similar age around Sydney seemed to contain a fossil dead zone. There were no leaves or roots and scarcely a fossil of any kind, with one critical exception: simple, curved sand-filled burrows up to two meters long. Based on the sizes and shapes of these burrows, we concluded that they were most likely excavated by small mammal-like reptiles roughly the size of modern gophers or mole rats. The busy burrowers had made their homes in the muddy dead zone, implying that these animals had survived the end-Permian catastrophe. Moreover, their burrowing strategy was probably key to their success: it provided a refuge from the scorching surface.

All organisms must bend to the forces of nature. Like our ancestors that survived the end-Permian event, we sought a reprieve from the punishing temperatures during our fieldwork. Fortunately, we had to hide for just a few hours before we could emerge. But what if the insufferable heat had lasted months— or millennia?

Before long the sun crept westward, casting us in the cliff's shadow, and we concluded the day's work by collecting more rock samples to analyze back in the laboratory. For most paleontologists, the absence of observable fossils, as occurs within the dead zone of a mass extinction, makes for a short expedition. But we suspected that the full story lay hidden in fossils that couldn't be seen with the naked eye.

We combined the day's samples with those we had collected from other rocks of the same age around Sydney, then split them into three batches. We sent one batch off to Jim Crowley of Boise State University and Bob Nicoll of Geoscience Australia to obtain precise age estimates for the extinction event. The second batch went to our colleague Tracy Frank of the University of Connecticut so she could calculate the temperatures that prevailed during the late Permian. We took the third batch with us to the Swedish Museum of Natural History, where we sifted through the samples for microscopic fossils of plant spores and pollen, as well as microbial algae and bacteria, to build a blow-by-blow account of the ecological collapse and recovery.

As expected, our analyses of the microfossils showed that abundances of plant spores and pollen dropped off precisely at the top of the last Permian coal deposit, reflecting near-total deforestation of the landscape. To our surprise, however, we also found that algae and bacteria had proliferated soon after the extinction, infesting freshwater ecosystems with noxious slime. In fact, they reached concentrations typical of modern microbial blooms, such as the record-breaking blooms in Lake Erie in 2011 and 2014. Because explosive microbial growth leads to poorly oxygenated waters, and many microbes produce metabolic by-products that are toxic, these events can cause animals to die en masse. In the wake of the end-Permian devastation, the humblest of organisms had inherited the lakes and rivers and established a new freshwater regime. We wondered how these microbes came to flourish to such a great extent and what the consequences of their burgeoning were. To answer these questions, we needed more context.

Insights came from analyses of the other two samples. The age estimates revealed that the ecosystem collapse coincided with the first rumblings of tremendous volcanic eruptions in a "large igneous province" known as the Siberian Traps, in what is now Russia. The term "volcanic" seems inadequate in this context; the volume of magma in the Siberian Traps was a whopping several million cubic kilometers. Thus, the Siberian Traps province is to a volcano as a tsunami is to a ripple in your bathtub. Studies have consistently implicated the Siberian Traps igneous event as the ultimate instigator of the end-Permian mass extinction, in large part because of the composition of the rocks in the area. Prior to this event, the rocks underneath Siberia were rich in coal, oil, and gas. When the Siberian Traps erupted, the heat of the intrusive magma vaporized these hydrocarbons into greenhouse gases, which were then emitted into the atmosphere. Atmospheric carbon dioxide levels increased sixfold as a result.

The timing lined up with Tracy's new geochemical temperature estimates, which revealed an increase of 10 to 14 degrees Celsius in the Sydney region. The age estimates also nailed down the duration of the observed changes in the Sydney area: the temperature spike and ecosystem collapse had occurred within tens of thousands of years. This geologically rapid change in conditions drove animals from temperate zones to extinction or compelled them to live part-time in the cooler temperatures underground. It also triggered the widespread microbial blooms we detected in our microfossil studies: the slime revolution had begun.

The ancient recipe for this toxic soup relied on three main ingredients: high carbon dioxide, high temperatures, and high nutrients. During the end-Permian event, the Siberian Traps provided the first two ingredients. Sudden deforestation created the third: when the trees were wiped out, the soils they once anchored bled freely into the rivers and lakes, providing all the nutrients that the aquatic microbes needed to multiply. In the absence of "scum-sucking" animals such as fish and invertebrates that would otherwise keep their numbers down, these microbes proliferated in fits and starts over the following 300 millennia. Once this new slime dynasty had established its reign, microbe concentrations at times became so high that they made the water toxic, preventing animals from recovering their preextinction diversity for perhaps millions of years. We had just discovered that freshwater, the last possible refuge during that apocalyptic time, was no refuge at all.

A Recurrent Symptom

Author Terry Pratchett once wrote of revolutions: "They always come around again. That's why they're called revolutions." Although the end-Permian was uniquely ruinous to life, it was probably just the end of a spectrum of warming-driven extinction events in Earth's history. If the environmental conditions that led to the end-Permian microbial blooms are typical for mass extinctions, then other ecological disasters of the past should reveal similar uprisings. Indeed, almost all past mass extinctions have been linked to rapid and sustained CO_2-driven warming. One might therefore expect to see similar, albeit less dramatic, microbial signatures for many other events.

From the precious little previously published data we found on freshwater systems during other mass extinctions, the pattern held up. So far, so good. But the best sign that we were onto something significant came when we placed the end-Permian event, along with the others, on a spectrum from least to most severe. The extinctions appeared to show a "dose- response relationship." This term is often used to describe the reaction of an organism to an external stimulus, such as a drug or a virus. If the stimulus is really the cause of a reaction, then you would expect a higher dose of it to cause a stronger response. When we applied this reasoning, we saw that the global severity of these microbial "infections" of freshwater ecosystems really seemed to have increased with higher doses of climate warming. The relatively mild warming events barely elicited a microbial response at all, whereas the severe climate change of the end-Permian gave rise to a metaphorical pandemic of aquatic microbes.

We then compared this pattern with the most famous mass extinction of all: the end-Cretaceous event that took place 66 million years ago and led to the loss of most large-bodied vertebrate groups, including the nonbird dinosaurs. In a matter of days some of the most awesome animals to walk the land, swim the seas, or fly the skies were snuffed out. Although massive volcanic eruptions are known to have occurred at this time, the majority of extinctions from this event are generally attributed to the impact of an asteroid at least 10 kilometers in diameter that struck an area off the coast of modern-day Mexico at a speed of up to 20 kilometers a second. The resultant global cloud of dust, soot, and aerosols may have inhibited the proliferation of photosynthetic microbes in the immediate aftermath of the event. Once the sun broke through, some microbes did multiply, but their reign was short-lived and relatively restricted, probably because of the modest increases in global CO_2 and temperature.

Without a simmering Earth to prop them up, we found, a new world order for microbes quickly breaks down. The contrasting microbial responses to magma- and asteroid-driven extinction events highlight the importance of high CO_2 and temperature for fueling harmful algal and bacterial blooms. This link between greenhouse

41

gas–driven warming and toxic microbial blooms is both satisfying and alarming: an elegant theory of freshwater mass extinction is emerging, but it may be simpler than we thought to cause widespread biodiversity loss—and it all seems to start with rapid CO_2 emissions.

On the Rise

Today humans are providing the ingredients for toxic microbial soup in generous amounts. The first two components—CO_2 and warming—are by-products of powering our modern civilization for nearly 200 years. Our species has been industriously converting underground hydrocarbons into greenhouse gases with far more efficiency than any volcano. The third ingredient—nutrients—we have been feeding into our waterways in the form of fertilizer runoff from agriculture, eroded soil from logging, and human waste from sewage mismanagement. Toxic blooms have increased sharply as a result. Their annual costs to fisheries, ecosystem services such as drinking water, and health are measured in the billions of dollars and are set to rise.

Wildfires can exacerbate this problem. In a warming world, droughts intensify, and outbreaks of fire become more common even in moisture-rich environments, such as the peat forests of Indonesia and the Pantanal wetlands of South America. Wildfires not only increase nutrient levels in water by exposing the soil and enhancing nutrient runoff into the streams, but they also throw immense quantities of soot and micronutrients into the atmosphere, which then land in oceans and waterways. Recent studies have identified algal blooms in freshwater streams of the western U.S. in the wake of major fire events. Farther afield, in the aftermath of the 2019–2020 Australian Black Summer wildfires, a widespread bloom of marine algae was detected downwind of the continent in the Southern Ocean.

Wildfire could have helped nourish aquatic microbes in the deep past too. Our investigation of the sediments above the coal seams around Sydney revealed abundant charcoal, a clear sign of widespread burning in the last vestiges of the Permian coal swamps. As in the modern examples, a combination of surface runoff and wildfire ash may well have led to nutrient influx into late-Permian waterways and the proliferation of deadly bacteria and algae.

These ancient mass extinctions hold lessons for the present and the future. Consider the following two premises of Earth system science. First, the atmosphere, hydrosphere, geosphere, and biosphere are linked. If one is significantly modified, the others will react in predictable ways. Second, this principle is as true today as it was throughout Earth's past. The Intergovernmental Panel on Climate Change (IPCC) applied this logic in its latest assessment of the causes and impacts of global warming.

Drawing on ice, rock, and fossil records, this consortium of more than 200 scientists concluded that the world has not experienced the present levels of CO_2 in more than 2 million years. In periods with such levels of CO_2 in the past, how high were sea levels? How did these conditions affect soil-weathering rates? How were the forests distributed? In other words, how did this difference in the air affect the oceans, land, and life? Our society should be desperate to answer such questions in relation to our modern CO_2 levels of 415 parts per million (ppm), not to mention 800 or 900 ppm, which is where the IPCC estimates we'll be by the year 2100 if the world continues to burn fossil fuels at the current rate. As CO_2 keeps rising, we need to look further back in time for clues about what to expect. The records of past extreme warming events are only becoming more relevant.

The analogy between the end-Permian event and today breaks down in at least two important ways, yet these discrepancies may not be as comforting as we might hope. For one thing, the pace of warming was probably different. Life struggles to cope with large environmental changes on short timescales, so perhaps the end-Permian event, the worst struggle in history, occurred much more quickly than modern warming. It is more likely that modern warming is much faster, however. Our team and others have shown that the sixfold increase in CO_2 during the end-Permian collapse happened over the course of perhaps tens of thousands of years. At business-as-usual rates, the IPCC projects the same increase in CO_2 concentration within hundreds, not thousands, of years.

A second strike against the analogy is the human element. Humans are becoming a force of nature, like a magma plume or a rock from space, but the diversity of ecological stressors they exert is unique in Earth's history. For this reason, we argue that extreme warming events from the past, such as the one that occurred at the end of the Permian, potentially provide a clear signal of the consequences of climate change. If we listen carefully enough, the fossils and rocks can tell us the results of warming alone, without additional, possibly confounding influences from humans such as nutrient influx from agriculture, deforestation via logging, or extinctions from poaching.

Here is the message these past events are telling us with increasing clarity: one can cause the extinction of a large number of species simply by rapidly releasing a lot of greenhouse gas. It does not matter where the gases come from—whether the source is volcanoes, airplanes, or coal-fired power plants, the results end up being the same. When we add to that mix the myriad other stressors generated by humans, the long-term forecast for biodiversity seems bleak.

There is, however, a third way in which our species could break the analogy, one that is far more hopeful. Unlike the species that suffered the mass extinctions of the past, we can prevent biodiversity loss through the intelligent application of our ideas and our technologies. Case in point: we can prevent a microbial takeover by keeping our waterways clean and curbing our greenhouse gas emissions.

It is increasingly clear that we are living through the sixth major mass extinction. Freshwater microbial blooms, wildfires, coral bleaching, and spikes in ocean temperature are becoming more frequent and intense in our warming world. Where along the extinction-event spectrum the present warming will place us is, for the first time in Earth's history, up to just one species.

About the Authors

Chris Mays is a lecturer in paleontology at University College Cork in Ireland. His research focuses on mass extinctions and how polar plants and animals responded to warming events in the past.

Vivi Vajda is a geologist at the Swedish Museum of Natural History who specializes in microscopic fossils, including those of plankton and algae. She studies vegetation changes through time to better understand mass extinctions.

Stephen McLoughlin is curator of the Paleozoic and Mesozoic plant fossil collections at the Swedish Museum of Natural History. His research interests revolve around the evolution and extinction of plant life on Earth.

Section 3: Pandemic Threats

Stopping Deforestation Can Prevent Pandemics

By the Editors of *Scientific American*

S ARS, Ebola, and now SARS-CoV-2: all three of these highly infectious viruses have caused global panic since 2002—and all three of them jumped to humans from wild animals that live in dense tropical forests.

Three quarters of the emerging pathogens that infect humans leaped from animals, many of them creatures in the forest habitats that we are slashing and burning to create land for crops, including biofuel plants, and for mining and housing. The more we clear, the more we come into contact with wildlife that carries microbes well suited to kill us—and the more we concentrate those animals in smaller areas where they can swap infectious microbes, raising the chances of novel strains. Clearing land also reduces biodiversity, and the species that survive are more likely to host illnesses that can be transferred to humans. All these factors will lead to more spillover of animal pathogens into people.

Stopping deforestation will not only reduce our exposure to new disasters but also tamp down the spread of a long list of other vicious diseases that have come from rain forest habitats—Zika, Nipah, malaria, cholera, and HIV among them. A 2019 study found that a 10 percent increase in deforestation would raise malaria cases by 3.3 percent; that would be 7.4 million people worldwide. Yet despite years of global outcry, deforestation still runs rampant. An average of 28 million hectares of forest have been cut down annually since 2016, and there is no sign of a slowdown.

Societies can take numerous steps to prevent the destruction. Eating less meat, which physicians say will improve our health anyway, will lessen demand for crops and pastures. Eating fewer processed foods will reduce the demand for palm oil—also a major feedstock for biofuels—much of which is grown on land clear-cut from tropical rain forests. The need for land also will ease if nations slow population growth—something that can happen in developing nations only if women are given better education, equal social status with men, and easy access to affordable contraceptives.

Producing more food per hectare can boost supply without the need to clear more land. Developing crops that better resist drought will help, especially as climate change brings longer, deeper droughts. In dry regions of Africa and elsewhere, agroforestry techniques such as planting trees among farm fields can increase crop yields. Reducing food waste could also vastly lessen the pressure to grow more; 30 to 40 percent of all food produced is wasted.

As we implement these solutions, we can also find new outbreaks earlier. Epidemiologists want to tiptoe into wild habitats and test mammals known to carry coronaviruses—bats, rodents, badgers, civets, pangolins and monkeys—to map how the germs are moving. Public health officials could then test nearby humans. To be effective, though, this surveillance must be widespread and well funded. In September 2019, just months before the COVID-19 pandemic began, the U.S. Agency for International Development announced it would end funding for PREDICT, a 10-year effort to hunt for threatening microbes that found more than 1,100 unique viruses. USAID says it will launch a new surveillance program; we urge it to supply enough money this time to cast a wider and stronger net.

In the meantime, governments should prohibit the sale of live wild animals in so-called wet markets, where pathogens have repeatedly crossed over into humans. The markets may be culturally important, but the risk is too great. Governments must also crack down on illegal wildlife trade, which can spread infectious agents far and wide. In addition, we have to examine factory farms that pack thousands of animals together—the source of the 2009 swine flu outbreak that killed more than 10,000 people in the U.S. and multitudes worldwide.

Ending deforestation and thwarting pandemics would address six of the United Nations' 17 Sustainable Development Goals: the guarantee of healthy lives, zero hunger, gender equality, responsible consumption and production, sustainably managed land, and climate

48

action (intact tropical forests absorb carbon dioxide, whereas burning them sends more CO_2 into the atmosphere).

The COVID-19 pandemic is a catastrophe, but it can rivet our attention on the enormous payoffs that humanity can achieve by not overexploiting the natural world. Pandemic solutions are sustainability solutions.

Deadly Fungi Are the Newest Emerging Microbe Threat All Over the World

By Maryn McKenna

I t was the fourth week of June in 2020, and the middle of the second wave of the COVID pandemic in the U.S. Cases had passed 2.4 million; deaths from the novel coronavirus were closing in on 125,000. In his home office in Atlanta, Tom Chiller looked up from his emails and scrubbed his hands over his face and shaved head.

Chiller is a physician and an epidemiologist and, in normal times, a branch chief at the U.S. Centers for Disease Control and Prevention, in charge of the section that monitors health threats from fungi such as molds and yeasts. He had put that specialty aside in March when the U.S. began to recognize the size of the threat from the new virus, when New York City went into lockdown and the CDC told almost all of its thousands of employees to work from home. Ever since, Chiller had been part of the public health agency's frustrating, stymied effort against COVID. Its employees had been working with state health departments, keeping tabs on reports of cases and deaths and what jurisdictions needed to do to stay safe.

Shrugging off exhaustion, Chiller focused on his in-box again. Buried in it was a bulletin forwarded by one of his staff that made him sit up and grit his teeth. Hospitals near Los Angeles that were handling an onslaught of COVID were reporting a new problem: Some of their patients had developed additional infections, with a fungus called *Candida auris*. The state had gone on high alert.

Chiller knew all about *C. auris*—possibly more about it than anyone else in the U.S. Almost exactly four years earlier he and the CDC had sent an urgent bulletin to hospitals, telling them to be on the lookout. The fungus had not yet appeared in the U.S., but Chiller had been chatting with peers in other countries and had heard what happened when the microbe invaded their health-care systems. It resisted treatment by most of the few drugs that could

50

be used against it. It thrived on cold hard surfaces and laughed at cleaning chemicals; some hospitals where it landed had to rip out equipment and walls to defeat it. It caused fast-spreading outbreaks and killed up to two thirds of the people who contracted it.

Shortly after that warning, *C. auris* did enter the U.S. Before the end of 2016, 14 people contracted it, and four died. Since then, the CDC had been tracking its movement, classifying it as one of a small number of dangerous diseases that doctors and health departments had to tell the agency about. By the end of 2020 there had been more than 1,500 cases in the U.S., in 23 states. And then COVID arrived, killing people, overwhelming hospitals, and redirecting all public health efforts toward the new virus and away from other rogue organisms.

But from the start of the pandemic, Chiller had felt uneasy about its possible intersection with fungal infections. The first COVID case reports, published by Chinese scientists in international journals, described patients as catastrophically ill and consigned to intensive care: pharmaceutically paralyzed, plugged into ventilators, threaded with I.V. lines, loaded with drugs to suppress infection and inflammation. Those frantic interventions might save them from the virus—but immune-damping drugs would disable their innate defenses, and broad-spectrum antibiotics would kill off beneficial bacteria that keep invading microbes in check. Patients would be left extraordinarily vulnerable to any other pathogen that might be lurking nearby.

Chiller and his colleagues began quietly reaching out to colleagues in the U.S. and Europe, asking for any warning signs that COVID was allowing deadly fungi a foothold. Accounts of infections trickled back from India, Italy, Colombia, Germany, Austria, Belgium, Ireland, the Netherlands, and France. Now the same deadly fungi were surfacing in American patients as well: the first signs of a second epidemic, layered on top of the viral pandemic. And it wasn't just *C. auris*. Another deadly fungus called *Aspergillus* was starting to take a toll as well.

"This is going to be widespread everywhere," Chiller says. "We don't think we're going to be able to contain this."

We are likely to think of fungi, if we think of them at all, as minor nuisances: mold on cheese, mildew on shoes shoved to the back of the closet, mushrooms springing up in the garden after hard rains. We notice them, and then we scrape them off or dust them away, never perceiving that we are engaging with the fragile fringes of a web that knits the planet together. Fungi constitute their own biological kingdom of about 6 million diverse species, ranging from common companions such as baking yeast to wild exotics. They differ from the other kingdoms in complex ways. Unlike animals, they have cell walls; unlike plants, they cannot make their own food; unlike bacteria, they hold their DNA within a nucleus and pack cells with organelles—features that make them, at the cellular level, weirdly similar to us. Fungi break rocks, nourish plants, seed clouds, cloak our skin, and pack our guts, a mostly hidden and unrecorded world living alongside us and within us.

That mutual coexistence is now tipping out of balance. Fungi are surging beyond the climate zones they long lived in, adapting to environments that would once have been inimical, learning new behaviors that let them leap between species in novel ways. While executing those maneuvers, they are becoming more successful pathogens, threatening human health in ways—and numbers—they could not achieve before.

Surveillance that identifies serious fungal infections is patchy, and so any number is probably an undercount. But one widely shared estimate proposes that there are possibly 300 million people infected with fungal diseases worldwide and 1.6 million deaths every year—more than malaria, as many as tuberculosis. Just in the U.S., the CDC estimates that more than 75,000 people are hospitalized annually for a fungal infection, and another 8.9 million people seek an outpatient visit, costing about $7.2 billion a year.

For physicians and epidemiologists, this is surprising and unnerving. Long-standing medical doctrine holds that we are protected from fungi not just by layered immune defenses but because we are mammals, with core temperatures higher than fungi prefer. The cooler outer surfaces of our bodies are at risk of minor assaults—think of athlete's foot, yeast infections, ringworm—but in people with healthy immune systems, invasive infections have been rare.

That may have left us overconfident. "We have an enormous blind spot," says Arturo Casadevall, a physician and molecular microbiologist at the Johns Hopkins Bloomberg School of Public Health. "Walk into the street and ask people what are they afraid of, and they'll tell you they're afraid of bacteria, they're afraid of viruses, but they don't fear dying of fungi."

Ironically, it is our successes that made us vulnerable. Fungi exploit damaged immune systems, but before the mid-20th century people with impaired immunity didn't live very long. Since then, medicine has gotten very good at keeping such people alive, even though their immune systems are compromised by illness or cancer treatment or age. It has also developed an array of therapies that deliberately suppress immunity, to keep transplant recipients healthy and treat autoimmune disorders such as lupus and rheumatoid arthritis. So vast numbers of people are living now who are especially vulnerable to fungi. (It was a fungal infection, *Pneumocystis carinii* pneumonia, that alerted doctors to the first known cases of HIV 40 years ago this June.)

Not all of our vulnerability is the fault of medicine preserving life so successfully. Other human actions have opened more doors between the fungal world and our own. We clear land for crops and settlement and perturb what were stable balances between fungi and their hosts. We carry goods and animals across the world, and fungi hitchhike on them. We drench crops in fungicides and enhance the resistance of organisms residing nearby. We take actions that warm the climate, and fungi adapt, narrowing the gap between their preferred temperature and ours that protected us for so long.

But fungi did not rampage onto our turf from some foreign place. They were always with us, woven through our lives and our environments and even our bodies: every day, every person on the planet inhales at least 1,000 fungal spores. It is not possible to close ourselves off from the fungal kingdom. But scientists are urgently trying to understand the myriad ways in which we

53

dismantled our defenses against the microbes, to figure out better approaches to rebuild them.

It is perplexing that we humans have felt so safe from fungi when we have known for centuries that our crops can be devastated from their attacks. In the 1840s a funguslike organism, *Phytophthora infestans*, destroyed the Irish potato crop; more than 1 million people, one eighth of the population, starved to death. (The microbe, formerly considered a fungus, is now classified as a highly similar organism, a water mold.) In the 1870s coffee leaf rust, *Hemileia vastatrix*, wiped out coffee plants in all of South Asia, completely reordering the colonial agriculture of India and Sri Lanka and transferring coffee production to Central and South America. Fungi are the reason that billions of American chestnut trees vanished from Appalachian forests in the U.S. in the 1920s and that millions of dying Dutch elms were cut out of American cities in the 1940s. They destroy one fifth of the world's food crops in the field every year.

Yet for years medicine looked at the devastation fungi wreak on the plant kingdom and never considered that humans or other animals might be equally at risk. "Plant pathologists and farmers take fungi very seriously and always have, and agribusiness has," says Matthew C. Fisher, a professor of epidemiology at Imperial College London, whose work focuses on identifying emerging fungal threats. "But they're very neglected from the point of view of wildlife disease and also human disease."

So when the feral cats of Rio de Janeiro began to fall ill, no one at first thought to ask why. Street cats have hard lives anyway, scrounging, fighting and birthing endless litters of kittens. But in the summer of 1998, dozens and then hundreds of neighborhood cats began showing horrific injuries: weeping sores on their paws and ears, clouded swollen eyes, what looked like tumors blooming out of their faces. The cats of Rio live intermingled with humans: Children play with them, and especially in poor neighborhoods women encourage them to stay near houses and deal with rats and mice. Before long some of the kids and mothers started to get sick as well. Round, crusty-edge wounds opened on their hands, and hard red lumps trailed up their arms as though following a track.

In 2001 researchers at the Oswaldo Cruz Foundation, a hospital and research institute located in Rio, realized they had treated 178 people in three years, mostly mothers and grandmothers, for similar lumps and oozing lesions. Almost all of them had everyday contact with cats. Analyzing the infections and ones in cats treated at a nearby vet clinic, they found a fungus called *Sporothrix*.

The various species of the genus *Sporothrix* live in soil and on plants. Introduced into the body by a cut or scratch, this fungus transforms into a budding form resembling a yeast. In the past, the yeast form had not been communicable, but in this epidemic, it was. That was how the cats were infecting one another and their caretakers: Yeasts in their wounds and saliva flew from cat to cat when they fought or jostled or sneezed. Cats passed it to humans via claws and teeth and caresses. The infections spread from skin up into lymph nodes and the bloodstream and to eyes and internal organs. In case reports amassed by doctors in Brazil, there were accounts of fungal cysts growing in people's brains.

The fungus with this skill was decreed a new species, *Sporothrix brasiliensis*. By 2004, 759 people had been treated for the disease at the Cruz Foundation; by 2011, the count was up to 4,100 people. By last year, more than 12,000 people in Brazil had been diagnosed with the disease across a swath of more than 2,500 miles. It has spread to Paraguay, Argentina, Bolivia, Colombia, and Panama.

"This epidemic will not take a break," says Flávio Queiroz-Telles, a physician and associate professor at the Federal University of Paraná in Curitiba, who saw his first case in 2011. "It is expanding."

It was a mystery how: Feral cats wander, but they do not migrate thousands of miles. At the CDC, Chiller and his colleagues suspected a possible answer. In Brazil and Argentina, sporotrichosis has been found in rats as well as cats. Infected rodents could hop rides on goods that move into shipping containers. Millions of those containers land on ships docking at American ports every day.

The fungus could be coming to the U.S. A sick rat that escaped a container could seed the infection in the city surrounding a port.

"In dense population centers, where a lot of feral cats are, you could see an increase in extremely ill cats that are roaming the streets," says John Rossow, a veterinarian at the CDC, who may have been the first to notice the possible threat of *Sporothrix* to the U.S. "And being that we Americans can't avoid helping stray animals, I imagine we're going to see a lot of transmission to people."

To a mycologist such as Chiller, this kind of spread is a warning: The fungal kingdom is on the move, pressing against the boundaries, seeking any possible advantage in its search for new hosts. And that we, perhaps, are helping them. "Fungi are alive; they adapt," he says. Among their several million species, "only around 300 that we know of cause human disease—so far. That's a lot of potential for newness and differentness, in things that have been around for a billion years."

Torrence Irvin was 44 years old when his fungal troubles started. A big healthy man who had been an athlete in high school and college, he lives in Patterson, Calif., a quiet town in the Central Valley tucked up against U.S. Route 5. A little more than two years earlier Irvin had bought a house in a new subdivision and moved in with his wife, Rhonda, and their two daughters. He was a warehouse manager for the retailer Crate & Barrel and the announcer for local youth football games.

In September 2018 Irvin started to feel like he had picked up a cold he couldn't shake. He dosed himself with Nyquil, but as the weeks went on, he felt weak and short of breath. On a day in October, he collapsed, falling to his knees in his bedroom. His daughter found him. His wife insisted they go to the emergency room.

Doctors thought he had pneumonia. They sent him home with antibiotics and instructions to use over-the-counter drugs. He got weaker and couldn't keep food down. He went to other doctors, while steadily getting worse, enduring shortness of breath, night sweats, and weight loss similar to a cancer victim's. From 280 pounds, he shrank to 150. Eventually one test turned up an answer: a fungal infection called coccidioidomycosis, usually known as Valley fever. "Until I got it, I had never heard of it," he says.

But others had. Irvin was referred to the University of California, Davis, 100 miles from his house, which had established a Center for Valley Fever. The ailment occurs mostly in California and Arizona, the southern tip of Nevada, New Mexico and far west Texas. The microbes behind it, *Coccidioides immitis* and *Coccidioides posadasii,* infect about 150,000 people in that area every year—and outside of the region the infection is barely known. "It's not a national pathogen—you don't get it in densely populated New York or Boston or D.C.," says George R. Thompson, co-director of the Davis center and the physician who began to supervise Irvin's care. "So even physicians view it as some exotic disease. But in areas where it's endemic, it's very common."

Similar to *Sporothrix*, *Coccidioides* has two forms, starting with a thready, fragile one that exists in soil and breaks apart when soil is disturbed. Its lightweight components can blow on the wind for hundreds of miles. Somewhere in his life in the Central Valley, Irvin had inhaled a dose. The fungus had transformed in his body into spheres packed with spores that migrated via his blood, infiltrating his skull and spine. To protect him, his body produced scar tissue that stiffened and blocked off his lungs. By the time he came under Thompson's care, seven months after he first collapsed, he was breathing with just 25 percent of his lung capacity. As life-threatening as that was, Irvin was nonetheless lucky: in about one case out of 100, the fungus grows life-threatening masses in organs and the membranes around the brain.

Irvin had been through all the approved treatments. There are only five classes of antifungal drugs, a small number compared with the more than 20 classes of antibiotics to fight bacteria. Antifungal medications are so few in part because they are difficult to design: because fungi and humans are similar at the cellular level, it is challenging to create a drug that can kill them without killing us too.

It is so challenging that a new class of antifungals reaches the market only every 20 years or so: the polyene class, including amphotericin B, in the 1950s; the azoles in the 1980s; and the echinocandin drugs, the newest remedy, beginning in 2001. (There is also terbinafine, used mostly for external infections, and flucytosine, used mostly in combination with other drugs.)

For Irvin, nothing worked well enough. "I was a skeleton," he recalls. "My dad would come visit and sit there with tears in his eyes. My kids didn't want to see me."

In a last-ditch effort, the Davis team got Irvin a new drug called olorofim. It is made in the U.K. and is not yet on the market, but a clinical trial was open to patients for whom every other drug had failed. Irvin qualified. Almost as soon as he received it, he began to turn the corner. His cheeks filled out. He levered himself to his feet with a walker. In several weeks, he went home.

Valley fever is eight times more common now than it was 20 years ago. That period coincides with more migration to the Southwest and West Coast—more house construction, more stirring up of soil—and also with increases in hot, dry weather linked to climate change. "*Coccidioides* is really happy in wet soil; it doesn't form spores, and thus it isn't particularly infectious," Thompson says. "During periods of drought, that's when the spores form. And we've had an awful lot of drought in the past decade."

Because Valley fever has always been a desert malady, scientists assumed the fungal threat would stay in those areas. But that is changing. In 2010 three people came down with Valley fever in eastern Washington State, 900 miles to the north: a 12-year-old who had been playing in a canyon and breathed the spores in, a 15-year-old who fell off an ATV and contracted Valley fever through his wounds, and a 58-year-old construction worker whose infection went to his brain. Research published two years ago shows such cases might become routine. Morgan Gorris, an earth systems scientist at Los Alamos National Laboratory, used climate-warming scenarios to project how much of the U.S. might become friendly territory for *Coccidioides* by the end of this century. In the scenario with the highest temperature rise, the area with conditions conducive to Valley fever—a mean annual temperature of 10.7 degrees Celsius (51 degrees Fahrenheit) and mean annual rainfall of less than

600 millimeters (23.6 inches)—reaches to the Canadian border and covers most of the western U.S.

Irvin has spent almost two years recovering; he still takes six pills of olorifim a day and expects to do that indefinitely. He gained back weight and strength, but his lungs remain damaged, and he has had to go on disability. "I am learning to live with this," he says. "I will be dealing with it for the rest of my life."

Sporothrix found a new way to transmit itself. Valley fever expanded into a new range. *C. auris*, the fungus that took advantage of COVID, performed a similar trick, exploiting niches opened by the chaos of the pandemic.

That fungus was already a bad actor. It did not behave the way that other pathogenic yeasts do, living quiescently in someone's gut and surging out into their blood or onto mucous membranes when their immune system shifted out of balance. At some point in the first decade of the century, *C. auris* gained the ability to directly pass from person to person. It learned to live on metal, plastic, and the rough surfaces of fabric and paper. When the first onslaught of COVID created a shortage of disposable masks and gowns, it forced health-care workers to reuse gear they usually discard between patients, to keep from carrying infections. And *C. auris* was ready.

In New Delhi, physician and microbiologist Anuradha Chowdhary read the early case reports and was unnerved that COVID seemed to be an inflammatory disease as much as a respiratory one. The routine medical response to inflammation would be to damp down the patient's immune response, using steroids. That would set patients up to be invaded by fungi, she realized. *C. auris*, lethal and persistent, had already been identified in hospitals in 40 countries on every continent except Antarctica. If health-care workers unknowingly carried the organism through their hospitals on reused clothing, there would be a conflagration.

"I thought, 'Oh, God, I.C.U.s are going to be overloaded with patients, and infection-control policies are going to be compromised,'" she said recently. "In any I.C.U. where *C. auris* is already present, it is going to play havoc."

Chowdhary published a warning to other physicians in a medical journal early in the pandemic. Within a few months she wrote an update: a 65 bed I.C.U. in New Delhi had been invaded by *C. auris*, and two thirds of the patients who contracted the yeast after they were admitted with COVID died. In the U.S., the bulletin that Chiller received flagged several hundred cases in hospitals and long-term care facilities in Los Angeles and nearby Orange County, and a single hospital in Florida disclosed that it harbored 35. Where there were a few, the CDC assumed that there were more—but that routine testing, their keyhole view into the organism's stealthy spread, had been abandoned under the overwork of caring for pandemic patients.

As bad as that was, physicians familiar with fungi were watching for a bigger threat: the amplification of another fungus that COVID might give an advantage to.

In nature, *Aspergillus* fumigatus serves as a clean-up crew. It encourages the decay of vegetation, keeping the world from being submerged in dead plants and autumn leaves. Yet in medicine, *Aspergillus* is known as the cause of an opportunistic infection spawned when a compromised human immune system cannot sweep away its spores. In people who are already ill, the mortality rate of invasive aspergillosis hovers near 100 percent.

During the 2009 pandemic of H1N1 avian flu, *Aspergillus* began finding new victims, healthy people whose only underlying illness was influenza. In hospitals in the Netherlands, a string of flu patients arrived unable to breathe and going into shock. In days, they died. By 2018 what physicians were calling invasive pulmonary aspergillosis was occurring in one out of three patients critically ill with flu and killing up to two thirds of them.

Then the coronavirus arrived. It scoured the interior lung surface the way flu does. Warning networks that link infectious disease doctors and mycologists around the globe lit up with accounts of aspergillosis taking down patients afflicted with COVID: in China, France, Belgium, Germany, the Netherlands, Austria, Ireland, Italy, and Iran. As challenging a complication as *C. auris* was, *Aspergillus* was worse. *C. auris* lurks in hospitals. The place where patients were exposed to *Aspergillus* was, well, everywhere. There was no way to eliminate the spores from the environment or keep people from breathing them in.

In Baltimore, physician Kieren Marr was acutely aware of the danger. Marr is a professor of medicine and oncology at Johns Hopkins Medical Center and directs its unit on transplant and oncology infectious diseases. The infections that take hold in people who have received a new organ or gotten a bone marrow transplant are familiar territory for her. When COVID arrived, she was concerned that *Aspergillus* would surge—and that U.S. hospitals, not alert to the threat, would miss it. Johns Hopkins began testing COVID patients in its ICU with the kind of molecular diagnostic tests used in Europe, trying to catch up to the infection in time to try to treat it. Across the five hospitals the Johns Hopkins system operates, it found that one out of 10 people with severe COVID was developing aspergillosis.

Several patients died, including one whose aspergillosis went to the brain. Marr feared there were many others like that patient, across the country, whose illness was not being detected in time. "This is bad," Marr said this spring. "*Aspergillus* is more important in COVID right now than *C. auris*. Without a doubt."

The challenge of countering pathogenic fungi is not only that they are virulent and sneaky, as bad as those traits may be. It is that fungi have gotten very good at protecting themselves against drugs we use to try to kill them.

The story is similar to that of antibiotic resistance. Drugmakers play a game of leapfrog, trying to get in front of the evolutionary maneuvers that bacteria use to protect themselves from drugs. For fungi, the tale is the same but worse. Fungal pathogens gain resistance against antifungal agents—but there are fewer drugs to start with, because the threat was recognized relatively recently.

"In the early 2000s, when I moved from academia to industry, the antifungal pipeline was zero," says John H. Rex, a physician and longtime advocate for antibiotic development. Rex is chief medical officer of F2G, which makes the not yet approved drug that Torrence

Irvin took. "There were no antifungals anywhere in the world in clinical or even preclinical development."

That is no longer the case, but research is slow; as with antibiotics, the financial rewards of bringing a new drug to market are uncertain. But developing new drugs is critical because patients may need to take them for months, sometimes for years, and many of the existing antifungals are toxic to us. (Amphotericin B gets called "shake and bake" for its grueling side effects.) "As a physician, you're making a choice to deal with a fungal infection at the cost of the kidney," says Ciara Kennedy, president and CEO of Amplyx Pharmaceuticals, which has a novel antifungal under development. "Or if I don't deal with the fungal infection, knowing the patient's going to die."

Developing new drugs also is critical because the existing ones are losing their effectiveness. Irvin ended up in the olorofim trial because his Valley fever did not respond to any available drugs. *C. auris* already shows resistance to drugs in all three major antifungal classes. *Aspergillus* has been amassing resistance to the antifungal group most useful for treating it, known as the azoles, because it is exposed to them so persistently. Azoles are used all across the world—not only in agriculture to control crop diseases but in paints and plastics and building materials. In the game of leapfrog, fungi are already in front.

The best counter to the ravages of fungi is not treatment but prevention: not drugs but vaccines. Right now no vaccine exists for any fungal disease. But the difficulty of treating patients long term with toxic drugs, combined with staggering case numbers, makes finding one urgent. And for the first time, one might be in sight if not in reach.

The reason that rates of Valley fever are not worse than they are, when 10 percent of the U.S. population lives in the endemic area, is that infection confers lifelong immunity. That suggests a vaccine might be possible—and since the 1940s researchers have been trying. A prototype that used a killed version of the form *Coccidioides* takes inside the body—fungal spheres packed with spores—worked brilliantly in mice. But it failed dismally in humans in a clinical trial in the 1980s.

"We did it on a shoestring, and everyone wanted it to work," says John Galgiani, now a professor and director of the Valley Fever Center for Excellence at the University of Arizona College of Medicine, who was part of that research 40 years ago. "Even with [bad] reactions and the study lasting three years, we kept 95 percent of the people who enrolled."

Enter dogs. They have their noses in the dirt all the time, and that puts them at more risk of Valley fever than humans are. In several Arizona counties, close to 10 percent of dogs come down with the disease every year, and they are more likely to develop severe lung-blocking forms than human are. They suffer terribly, and it is lengthy and expensive to treat them. But dogs' vulnerability—plus the lower standards that federal agencies require to approve animal drugs compared with human ones—makes them a model system for testing a possible vaccine. And the passion of owners for their animals and their willingness to empty their wallets when they can may turn possibility into reality for the first time.

Galgiani and his Arizona group are now working on a new vaccine formula, thanks to financial donations from hundreds of dog owners, plus a boost from a National Institutes of Health grant and commercial assistance from a California company, Anivive Lifesciences. Testing is not complete, but it could reach the market for use in dogs as early as next year. "I think this is proof of concept for a fungal vaccine—having it in use in dogs, seeing it is safe," says Lisa Shubitz, a veterinarian and research scientist at the Arizona center. "I really believe this is the path to a human vaccine."

This injection does not depend on a killed Valley fever fungus. Instead it uses a live version of the fungus from which a gene that is key to its reproductive cycle, CPS1, has been deleted. The loss means the fungi are unable to spread. The gene was discovered by a team of plant pathologists and later was identified in *Coccidioides* by Marc Orbach of the University of Arizona, who studies host-pathogen interactions. After creating a mutant *Coccidioides* with the gene removed, he and Galgiani experimentally infected lab mice bred to be exquisitely sensitive to the fungus. The microbe provoked a strong immune reaction, activating type 1 T helper cells, which establish durable immunity. The mice survived for six months and did not develop any Valley fever symptoms, even though the team tried to infect them with unaltered *Coccidioides*. When the researchers autopsied the mice at the end of that half-year period, scientists found almost no fungus growing in their lungs. That long-lasting protection against infection makes the gene-deleted fungus the most promising basis for a vaccine since Galgiani's work in the 1980s. But turning a vaccine developed for dogs into one that could be used in humans will not be quick.

The canine formula comes under the purview of the U.S. Department of Agriculture, but approval of a human version would be overseen by the U.S. Food and Drug Administration. It would require clinical trials that would probably stretch over years and involve thousands of people rather than the small number of animals used to validate the formula in dogs. Unlike the 1980s prototype, the new vaccine involves a live organism. Because there has never been a fungal vaccine approved, there is no preestablished evaluation pathway for the developers or regulatory agencies to follow. "We would be flying the plane and building it at the same time," Galgiani says.

He estimates achieving a Valley fever vaccine for people could take five to seven years and about $150 million, an investment made against an uncertain promise of earnings. But a successful compound could have broad usefulness, protecting permanent residents of the Southwest as well as the military personnel at 120 bases and other installations in the endemic area, plus hundreds of thousands of "snowbird" migrants who visit every winter. (Three years ago the CDC identified cases of Valley fever in 14 states outside the endemic zone. Most were in wintertime inhabitants of the Southwest who were diagnosed after they went back home.) By one estimate, a vaccine could save potentially $1.5 billion in health-care costs every year.

"I couldn't see the possibility that we'd have a vaccine 10 years ago," Galgiani says. "But I think it is possible now."

If one fungal vaccine is achieved, it would carve the path for another. If immunizations were successful—scientifically, as targets of regulation and as vaccines people would be willing to accept—

we would no longer need to be on constant guard against the fungal kingdom. We could live alongside and within it, safely and confidently, without fear of the ravages it can wreak.

But that is years away, and fungi are moving right now: changing their habits, altering their patterns, taking advantage of emergencies such as COVID to find fresh victims. At the CDC, Chiller is apprehensive.

"The past five years really felt like we were waking up to a whole new phenomenon, a fungal world that we just weren't used to," Chiller says. "How do we stay on top of that? How do we question ourselves to look for what might come next? We study these emergences not as an academic exercise but because they show us what might be coming. We need to be prepared for more surprises."

About the Author

Maryn McKenna is a journalist specializing in public health, global health and food policy and a senior fellow of the Center for the Study of Human Health at Emory University. She is author most recently of Big Chicken: The Incredible Story of How Antibiotics Created Modern Agriculture and Changed the Way the World Eats *(National Geographic Books, 2017).*

How Mathematics Can Predict—And Help Prevent—The Next Pandemic

By Rachel Crowell

P redicting and understanding disease outbreaks doesn't just involve epidemiology. It takes math too. For centuries mathematicians have tackled questions related to epidemics and pandemics, along with potential responses to them. For instance, 18th-century Swiss mathematician Daniel Bernoulli is credited with developing the first mathematical epidemiology model, which focused on analyzing the effects of smallpox inoculation on life expectancy. Mathematicians have continued this work to the present day, including during the COVID pandemic.

One such researcher is Abba Gumel, a mathematician and mathematical biologist at the University of Maryland, College Park. He was recently elected to the current class of fellows of the American Association for the Advancement of Science (AAAS). Mathematicians such as him are indispensable to the mission of identifying and averting the next pandemic. Succeeding in this quest, however, requires that they unite with experts from other fields and work together to solve these multifaceted disease-transmission problems.

Gumel spoke to *Scientific American* about how he is using mathematics to combat infectious diseases and about the questions he hopes to address before the next pandemic hits.

[An edited transcript of the interview follows.]

Q: Tell me about a time that one of your recent findings surprised you.

A: We showed in our paper on COVID lockdown measures that the number of cases, hospitalizations and mortality would have been dramatically reduced if we had started community lockdowns a week or two earlier than we did. This means hitting the disease hard early, before it enters the exponential phase of transmission.

It would have dramatically altered the course of the pandemic in the U.S. and perhaps saved hundreds of thousands of lives.

Q: What role can mathematicians play in preventing the next pandemic?

A: What mathematicians are doing to help prevent the next one is basically working on lessons we have learned. We have learned that masks worked from mathematical analysis and modeling but also from what happened in society. Societies that have high coverage of masks and high-quality masks did well in reducing cases and mortality. Vaccines work, we have shown clearly, if we raise the level of herd immunity required. For the next pandemic, if we have certain vaccines with starting efficacies, we can predict the minimum proportion we need to vaccinate to achieve vaccine-induced herd immunity.

We're coming up with this bucket list of things to do to prevent, we hope, the next one but even if we do get hit—and we're going to get hit—to minimize the burden of the next one and to greatly suppress it before it becomes a problem. These are things we need to do to make sure the next one doesn't kill 1 million Americans.

Sometimes when I talk about it, I cry because I see that if we had done the right thing, none of this would have happened.

Q: What are some pressing open questions you hope to address before the next pandemic hits?

A: I am interested in determining whether stockpiling high-quality face masks and making them widely available early in a new COVID-like pandemic can obviate the need to shut down the economy until a safe and effective vaccine becomes available.

I am interested in determining the impact of increases in global temperature caused by global warming on the population and distribution of wild animal populations and associated viral zoonotic diseases and the likelihood of a spillover event.

I am also interested in quantifying the burden of a potential highly contagious and highly fatal pandemic of a contact-based disease such as Ebola viral disease. The world community thankfully averted such a catastrophe when we came together and effectively contained the Ebola outbreaks that took place in Guinea, Liberia, and Sierra Leone in 2014–2016.

Q: **Before the COVID pandemic, you mainly focused on mosquito-borne diseases. Are there fundamental differences in how you approach studying infectious diseases such as malaria that involve a vector?**

A: Yes, there's a big difference. There's no direct human-to-human transmission. Mosquitoes get infected by biting infectious humans. If I'm infected and a mosquito takes a blood meal from me, there's some probability that the mosquito can also get my *Plasmodium* parasite and become infected. So the modeling types are different.

West Nile is transmitted by mosquitoes not only to humans but also to other hosts such as crows. But the birds fly long distances, so we use spatial models.

Q: **What are some other factors that affect your modeling decisions?**

A: The type of model you choose depends on the level of data you have. An agent-based model allows you to track each individual: their risk of getting infected, what they do each day, and all that. That's very useful in determining who infected whom. But it's data-hungry. You need a lot of data at an individual level.

The type of model you choose depends on the problem you want to solve, the type of data you have and the quality of the data.

Q: **What does your selection as an AAAS Fellow mean to you?**

A: It's a huge honor. And the honor belongs to the large number of people in my support network.

This gives me an additional platform to multiply my efforts in community outreach. I've been focused on Africa and other developing regions of the world to provide opportunities for people to be the best they can become in STEM [science, technology, engineering and mathematics]. I'm focused on young people, especially women. I'm focused on getting a lot more women in rural areas to get into STEM and be among the best. I'm very worried about gender inequity. I'm doing whatever I can to bridge that gap. Particularly, where I came from in Africa [Nigeria], we need a lot more women in STEM.

We have a tremendous responsibility. We need to make science accessible to everyone around the world. It doesn't work at all if only a few countries are scientifically advanced. Look at what's happened. COVID started in China, but it became a problem for everyone.

We're all vulnerable to what's happening in faraway places—the same with inequity in STEM, inequity in health care, inequity in economics. If we're doing well, but our neighbor is not, it's just a matter of time before we also suffer. It's the same thing with viral things happening in faraway places. We had better pay attention because it's a plane ride away from coming to us.

About the Author

Rachel Crowell is a Midwest-based writer covering science and mathematics. Follow Crowell on X (formerly Twitter) @writesRCrowell.

Section 4: Asteroid Impacts

Are We Doing Enough to Protect Earth from Asteroids?

By Sarah Scoles

In the first few seconds of video taken at the Arecibo radio telescope on December 1, 2020, everything looks normal. Sure, support cables had broken the previous August and November, damaging the 300-meter-wide dish. And *sure*, the National Science Foundation was already planning to decommission Arecibo, an instrument that began scanning the sky in 1963. So things weren't great for the telescope. But it was at least still there.

That changed just before 8 a.m. when, as if on command, a bit of dust puffed out from a support pillar. That was, it turns out, a cable beginning to snap off. Left with extra load, other cables began to break, too. Soon the massive equipment platform, once suspended over the bowl-shaped observatory, began to tip. After an agonizing swing downward, the platform crashed. More cables snapped, and debris flew around like in a demolition. At the end of the footage, giant holes were visible in the iconic telescope, and dust rose all around. Arecibo, at least as scientists knew it, was gone.

When Edgard Rivera-Valentín, a staff scientist at the Lunar and Planetary Institute and formerly part of the planetary radar group at Arecibo, clicked on the video, they could stomach only a few seconds. It took them days to get through the full two minutes. "When everything went down, it was—I use the word 'tragedy,' " says Rivera-Valentín, a native of Puerto Rico.

Arecibo had a long and storied legacy of scientific discovery, studying space weather, searching for extraterrestrials, timing pulsars, mapping neutral hydrogen gas. But it also had an unconventional claim to fame: It boasted the world's most powerful, sensitive and active planetary radar system. That radar could peer through Venus's thick atmosphere and map the dusty Martian surface, but it also helped protect Earth from asteroids. The data showed scientists

71

those rocks in detail, revealed whether they might present a threat, and helped humans figure out what they could reasonably do if an asteroid was heading our way. "One of the neat things about doing radar is that you're actively defending the entire Earth," Rivera-Valentín says. "So if anyone asks you, 'Why should I care?,' it's like, 'I'm going to make sure that asteroid doesn't come for you.'"

Arecibo's radar efforts fell under the umbrella of "planetary defense": the attempt to identify and prevent potential collisions between asteroids (and comets) and this planet, which, ideally, we would like to keep intact.

On any given day the likelihood is low that a space rock will devastatingly smash into Earth. But the consequences of such a catastrophe would be severe. And our solar system's history—planets pocked with craters, crashes on other planets in recent memory, huge objects hurtling through Earth's atmosphere and captured on dashcams—demonstrates the statistical truth that events unlikely to happen on any given day do happen, given enough days. That's why NASA has an entire office dedicated to the problem; why a slew of astronomical facilities gather preventive data; and why an upcoming space mission will demonstrate what earthlings can do if a space rock does come knocking.

But is it enough? With Arecibo and its radar out of commission, our planetary defense arsenal comes up short. The U.S. and other nations are assessing the risk, brainstorming new ways to stay ahead of the threat and formulating plans for what might come next.

Counting Space Rocks

Planetary defense has been plagued by a "giggle factor." After all, apocalypse by asteroid seems the stuff of feature films, not serious science. But officials started to pay more attention soon after a comet called Shoemaker-Levy headed straight for Jupiter in 1994. Linda Billings, a consultant for NASA's planetary defense communications efforts, remembers when the two collided. On July 21, 1994—a few days into a series of impacts—she went to an open house at the

Naval Observatory in Washington, D.C., where sky watchers could spy on Jupiter. On the lawn outside, amateur astronomers trained their own instruments on the scarred planet. Jupiter's gravity had shredded the comet into pieces, which streamed into the planet's swirling atmosphere, reaching 40,000 degrees Celsius and sending 3,000-kilometer-high plumes of material shooting into space. "We had solid evidence that impacts occur," Billings says, understatedly.

Soon after, U.S. Air Force officials published two reports, *SpaceCast 2020* and *Air Force 2025*, on what the military could or should do to mitigate the threat of space rocks in the coming decades. Space impacts were a national security problem. The first report, meant to figure out how the U.S. could maintain the "high ground" in space, coined the term "planetary defense." The second had much the same goal, and both described asteroid detection and mitigation, the word for efforts to dispense with a threat if one arises—by, for instance, deflecting an asteroid by slamming into it with a spacecraft or exploding a nuclear weapon nearby.

Back then, scientists now well known for their planetary protection work were part of the air force—people such as Lindley Johnson, now program executive of NASA's Planetary Defense Coordination Office (and an author of the relevant part of *SpaceCast*), and Pete Worden, former director of NASA's Ames Research Center. They and their colleagues warned about the risk of civilization turning into a crater. But especially after 9/11, the issue did not receive as much attention as many would have liked. Johnson retired from active duty in 2003. "NASA said, 'Come on over. We've got a job for you,'" he says. One of his duties was to run NASA's Near-Earth Object Observations program. Today, in large part a result of Johnson's efforts, that has mushroomed into an entire Planetary Defense Coordination Office, where he is the boss. "An unwarned impact would be the biggest natural disaster we've ever seen, quite frankly," Johnson says. His office hopes to make any hypothetical impact an avoidable one.

To that end, NASA's office runs asteroid data-gathering programs, relying in part on wide-field optical and infrared telescopes that can see a broad expanse of the sky. Observatories run by the University of Arizona and the University of Hawaii have worked with Johnson's office to adapt their existing telescopes into sentries. The group also repurposed the space-based Wide Area Infrared Survey Explorer (WISE) into NEOWISE (Near-Earth Object WISE) in the years after it was initially decommissioned in 2011. NEOWISE recently completed its 14th all-sky survey and is working on its 15th.

Meanwhile M.I.T. Lincoln Laboratory's Lincoln Near-Earth Asteroid Research (LINEAR) software is currently installed on an air force asset called the Space Surveillance Telescope (SST) in Australia. The software makes this military observatory the world's most productive asteroid-hunting instrument, by some metrics. It has discovered 142 previously unknown near-Earth objects, four potentially hazardous objects, and eight new comets.

That's great but not as good as Congress would like. The official mandate these days is to discover 90 percent of the objects that are 140 meters or larger—the size at which a boom would result in "a pretty bad day anywhere," according to Johnson. There are an estimated 25,000 such baddies. "We are getting close, and maybe by the end of the year we'll have found 10,000 of those," he says. That is 40 percent completion for 20 years of effort. Overall, scientists have discovered more than 25,000 near-Earth asteroids of any size, and around 19,000 of those caught on camera are bigger than 30 meters.

Replacing Arecibo

Globally, 30 space organizations—based everywhere from Latvia to Colombia, from China to Israel, and involving dedicated amateurs, national space agencies and individual observatories—participate in the International Asteroid Warning Network. The group, formed at the recommendation of the United Nations, coordinates observation and response efforts across our vulnerable planet. Since 2016 it has logged more than 300 close approaches, when asteroids were projected to come within one lunar distance—the average distance between Earth and the moon—of the globe's center. It has also coordinated three campaigns to practice "the observing resources and characterization capabilities that may be applied to a near-Earth object on a reasonably short timescale."

That is useful because the work is not finished when close-calling objects are discovered. Ground-based optical and infrared telescopes in places such as Hawaii, New Mexico, and Arizona make follow-up observations to learn more about the objects than the fact of their existence. Planetary radar, too, typically plays a role in refining the orbits of newly discovered asteroids and projecting their paths into the future—mapping out where those objects will go in the years to come and whether they might intersect with Earth. Radar also helps to discern asteroids' shape, composition, and trajectory.

Radar observations such as Arecibo's work like this: If you blast powerful radio waves toward the object, they bounce back, changed by the object's spin, motion, shape, and size, as well as by any moons the asteroid might have. The time they take to holler back also reveals the object's precise distance from Earth. With all that information, you can refine its orbit and predict where it will be far into the future and whether that "where" includes Iowa. You can also learn about its properties—useful if you must knock it off course. Is it dense? Porous? Round? Peanutty? "When we record the echo that comes back, if it's different in any way from what we transmitted, we know that was due to the properties of the target, in this case, the asteroid," says Patrick Taylor, a senior staff scientist at the Lunar and Planetary Institute and former group lead for Arecibo's radar program.

Getting a radar observation is like taking a picture of the asteroid from the safety of the ground. "That is kind of like a flyby of a spacecraft at a tiny fraction of the cost," says Ellen Howell of the University of Arizona. "We get pictures of them as individual rocks, not just points of light." Which is significant, because as planetary scientists are fond of saying, if you've seen one asteroid, you've seen one asteroid. With the loss of Arecibo, Howell says, "that capability is now severely diminished." This ability to take observations of the present, predict the future and then *change* the future is what could set us apart from the poor saps of the past, who just had to take whatever knocks space sent their way. "Dinosaurs didn't have a space program," Rivera-Valentín says. "But we do."

Arecibo was not the only planetary radar in the U.S. There is one left—the Goldstone Solar System Radar in California—but it can detect less than half the near-Earth asteroids that Arecibo could. And even if Goldstone were the perfect instrument, stuff happens, and if it is down—as it was for around 18 months of maintenance just before Arecibo collapsed—this planet will have to fly through space without seeing as much as it previously did. "Losing Arecibo is going to make people think more about what that next-generation step will be," Taylor says. "Whatever that is, I don't know."

Scientists have ideas. Some would like to build Arecibo 2.0, synthesizing a number of smaller dishes in the same island spot to work together as one larger dish, thereby restoring radar capabilities. At Green Bank Observatory in West Virginia, scientists just did their own demo with defense contractor Raytheon, beaming a radar signal to the moon and receiving the bounce-back at antennas spread throughout the U.S. in the Very Long Baseline Array, which is operated from New Mexico. They hope this will pave the way for a setup with more oomph that could do asteroid work. "The Green Bank proposal for upgrade sounds terrific to me," Billings says. "But it's not yet funded."

And even if it were, Michael Nolan of the University of Arizona doubts that Green Bank could replace Arecibo's capabilities. Transmitting from one spot and picking up in another is a data-intensive approach, and doing both from Green Bank has its own issues. "I don't see any of the things I've seen so far being the workhorse system," he says. Arecibo's hypothetical replacement does not have funding either, for instance.

And the question of what to do is only the first hurdle. There is also the larger issue of who should do it. Some experts argue that the burden is too much for the scientific community to bear alone. Perhaps, they say, the task should fall to an organization with extensive experience in long-term planning and, more important, stable funding. In other words, the Department of Defense— specifically, its newly minted Space Force.

Stopping Asteroids

The Space Force, a new branch of the military that largely deals with satellites and their safety and security, aims to track objects large and small, from here to the moon, as international and commercial activity—satellites, spacecraft, orbital manufacturing systems, pay-as-you-go trips—ramps up. That general effort is called space situational awareness, and it is usually carried out by optical instruments and long-range radar. While that radar is monitoring the activity in orbit, it could also detect asteroids that happen to be zooming through space in the same direction as (but, it is hoped, much farther out than) a satellite. NASA and Space Force officials have been talking about collaborating on such a win-win system. "It is beyond just brainstorming, but we have not settled on a particular concept yet," says Johnson, noting that the discussions are ongoing. In 2020 the two organizations signed a memorandum of understanding, agreeing to work together on certain things—including both planetary defense and space situational awareness. The Space Force referred questions about the collaboration back to NASA.

Some, though, want to expand the idea of military involvement. Peter Garretson, a senior fellow at the American Foreign Policy Council and former director of Air University's Space Horizons Research Task Force, would like to see the military lead planetary defense efforts, particularly mitigation. "NASA is principally a science and exploration agency. In my view, this is clearly a defense mission," Garretson says. "You're not deflecting the asteroid for science."

And actually *no* federal organization is specifically tasked with deflecting asteroids. But people are working on it anyway. One agency steeped in the effort is the Department of Energy—you know, the one with the nukes. At Los Alamos National Laboratory, Cathy Plesko does asteroid mitigation research. She got into planetary defense by studying impact craters on Mars using computer models. "But how do you *stop* making a crater?" she wondered. One day a senior astrophysicist at the lab said he thought the same sorts of code she used to model the craters could be used to model asteroid mitigation: They would show how an asteroid would react if something impacted it—rather than if it impacted something. This was the very stoppage she was wondering about.

She began studying the problem, but the lab's efforts weren't extensive—until February 2013. That month a 20-meter-wide asteroid screamed through the atmosphere and exploded nearly 30 kilometers above Chelyabinsk Oblast in Russia with the force of around 450 kilotons of TNT, injuring 1,600 people. As with Shoemaker-Levy, officials opened their eyes wider. Plesko's team spooled up and, together with NASA, started scrambling to understand what physics problems they needed to solve to respond if something bigger and badder came along. That work begins with revealing what asteroids are made of, a surprisingly hard problem to which radar provides the best Earth-based solution. "Are they rubble piles? Are they kind of mud balls? Are they chunks of iron?" Plesko asks. "There's a lot of variety." That variety makes simulations difficult. If you are modeling a plane on a computer, you know exactly how dense it is and how it is shaped. "We don't have those specifications for asteroids and comets," she says. "That's something we have to figure out."

Today Plesko examines the plethora of possibilities to whisk different kinds of asteroids away from the globe. One option is called a gravity tractor. You fly as heavy a spacecraft as you can muster as close to a space rock as you can sidle. "Your spacecraft can sort of lure the asteroid or the comet off its original course over time," she says. But it requires decades of luring, and the technology, she estimates, will not be ready for a century or so.

Some scientists have looked at using lasers attached to small spacecraft to heat up material and vaporize it, throwing it off the surface and thus—every action resulting in another equal and opposite—pushing the asteroid in the other direction. More bluntly, one could also slam an asteroid with a spacecraft before it slams into Earth. Alternatively: Shine a mirror at it, focusing solar rays, until it sheds material. Move it with rockets. Paint it to change its thermal properties and thus its orbit. Plesko, being at the Department of

Energy, also studies the boomier menu choice: a "nuclear standoff burst." That means detonating a nuclear weapon close to a near-Earth object, transferring energy and throwing off some material. That deflects the rock just like the other techniques, only more, you know, emphatically. But studies on exploding bombs on or below the surface of an asteroid suggest that they might break up into smaller pieces that present their own problems. Either way, this option gets complicated quickly given the nature of nuclear bombs and the international ban on placing weapons of mass destruction in space. A country could use "prepping for asteroids" as an excuse for nuclear proliferation; furthermore, an asteroid is a global threat, but a single country would be using its own arsenal to fight it. "No one takes that lightly," Plesko says.

Every two years the global community stages a Dungeons-and-Dragons-style role-playing game, in which agencies act out their response to a fictional planetary defense scenario. Information about the "impact scenario" gets posted online ahead of time, with more revealed each day in PowerPoint-style briefings. In 2019, ahead of their arrival at the conference, participants knew a rock between 100 and 300 meters across had a 1 percent change of hitting Earth eight years in the future. By day three they knew it was 260 meters long and 140 meters wide, dead set on a straight course to Denver.

While the group developed a mission to deflect the problem object, a broken-off piece 60 meters across nonetheless set a course for Manhattan. The role players switched to disaster-dealing mode, looking at how to evacuate, what to do about chemical factories and nuclear plants, and what the economic fallout would look like. The gamers returned to the tabletop this year (via videoconference) to investigate an asteroid that could come calling in just six months. The entire exercise "gives a reality check on how long it takes to do things," Plesko says. It's not like in Hollywood, she adds, which goes more like, "An asteroid is discovered; let's launch the thing." Still, responding in a meaningful way is something humans can accomplish, even if more slowly than on-screen.

A Test Run

Soon an audacious mission will test our ability to move mountains in space. Due to launch in late 2021 or early 2022, DART—the Double Asteroid Redirection Test—will aim to demonstrate that we can change an asteroid's path like that of a wayward teen. Andrew Rivkin of the Johns Hopkins University Applied Physics Laboratory (APL), one of the mission's investigation team leads, started studying asteroids for the fundamental science—the "origins of the solar system" stuff. "No matter what you're trying to answer, it kind of comes back to asteroids somehow," he says. Plus, he adds, you can buy pieces of them on eBay.

Or you can build a spacecraft to shove one around, as Rivkin is now doing. DART will travel to the Didymos system, which has a large asteroid called Didymos and a small moon called Dimorphos. Then the spacecraft will slam into the moon, changing its orbit around its bigger sibling and thus the bigger sibling's motion around the sun. The 610-kilogram spacecraft will hit the 4.8-billion-kilogram ("small") Dimorphos at a speed of 6.58 kilometers per second, changing (scientists think) its orbital period by about 10 minutes. Because Dimorphos itself is the size of an asteroid that could endanger cities, scientists hope to see how well they can transfer momentum from a spacecraft to a space rock. It is the medium-sized mitigation option, midway between "you nuke it, or you hide in the basement," as Rivkin frames it. It is also preventing an impact by making an impact. The general technique would work in single-asteroid systems, too—you can slam a spacecraft into a loner—but scientists have a good reason for choosing a double system for this test: it is simple to measure how much you changed a moon's orbit because you can just watch it pass in front of the larger asteroid in real time.

Scientists will get their first view of the system—as a single pixel—about a month before the smashup in 2022. "That one pixel is what we're trying to guide toward," says Elena Adams of APL, the mission systems engineer. An hour before arrival, they will glimpse the moon and begin navigating toward it. "And then *bam*, we lose all contact, which is good," Adams says. It means things have gone boom. ("Somebody pays you to do that, right?" Adams exults. "You get to destroy a $250-million spacecraft!")

The team hopes that the Goldstone radar, as well as space telescopes, will also watch the show. "We hoped Arecibo would," Rivkin says sadly. The data gathered, then and after the fact, will be fed into future models that scientists such as Plesko use to determine how to respond to an actual asteroid threat. "Programs like DART, they're insurance in case we do find something," Rivkin says. People pay for fire insurance and flood insurance; they check their basements for radon. "We are hoping and expecting that the radon test won't find any radon and the house is not going to catch fire or flood, but we are kind of doing our due diligence."

Although Rivkin is glad people no longer think of planetary defense as a joke and instead can fathom the utility of cosmic insurance, he cautions against space rock anxiety. "If people are being kept up at night by asteroids, hopefully it's thinking about all the cool science," he says. It is that science, in fact—figuring out how to detect, track, project and characterize these lonesome travelers—that enables the whole of planetary defense. And planetary defense, in turn, enables humans to wrest some control from the cosmos. "This is the first time as a species we have the opportunity to prevent a natural disaster," Plesko says. "We can't stop a hurricane or prevent earthquakes. We can't just go superglue the San Andreas Fault shut." But stopping a planet killer? "If we needed to," she says, "I really do believe we could do this."

About the Author

Sarah Scoles is a Colorado-based science journalist, a contributing editor at Scientific American *and* Popular Science, *and a senior contributor at* Undark. *She is author of* Making Contact *(2017) and* They Are Already Here *(2020), both published by Pegasus Books. Her newest book is* Countdown: The Blinding Future of Nuclear Weapons *(Bold Type Books, 2024).*

NASA's DART Spacecraft Successfully Smacks a Space Rock—Now What?

By Jonathan O'Callaghan

An asteroid wiped out the dinosaurs; now Earthlings are fighting back. The sight of saurian fossils in most any science museum is a potent reminder that asteroids can threaten Earth as they swing around our sun, occasionally coming dangerously close to our planet—or, 66 million years ago, too close. Now scientists have tested a method that might save our planet from future doomsdays. In the past hour, NASA's Double Asteroid Redirection Test (DART) spacecraft crashed into a small asteroid called Dimorphos.

As DART's full name implies, this impact was no accident. It's meant to shift the space rock's trajectory by a tiny but noticeable amount—a change that observers will carefully confirm and track from afar with a plethora of ground- and space-based telescopes. In the future, if a dangerous asteroid is found on a collision course with Earth, we might use this same technique to nudge it off course and avert disaster. "We're not blowing up the Death Star," says Andy Rivkin, DART investigation team lead at the Johns Hopkins University Applied Physics Laboratory (APL), which runs the mission. "We're using the momentum from the spacecraft to change the orbit of the asteroid."

DART launched in November 2021 on a collision course with Dimorphos, a small asteroid 160 meters in size that orbits another asteroid, Didymos, that is almost five times larger. Over nearly a year the vending-machine-sized, circa 600-kilogram spacecraft caught up to the asteroids, taking ever sharper images as it approached. That was until today, at 7:15 p.m. ET, when engineers at APL's mission control stopped receiving signals from the spacecraft, confirming its self-destructive slam into Dimorphos about 11 million kilometers from Earth.

"We are embarking on a new era for humankind," said Lori Glaze, director of NASA's planetary science division, in postimpact remarks during the space agency's live stream of the event, "an era in which we have the potential capability to protect ourselves from something like a dangerous asteroid impact."

Traveling at about 23,000 kilometers per hour, the spacecraft hit the asteroid with the approximate energy of three metric tons of TNT, exploding in a superheated shower of metal and asteroid debris. A small Italian spacecraft called LICIACube (Light Italian Cubesat for Imaging of Asteroids) following three minutes behind took images of the impact that will be released in the coming days. Yet the true mission has just begun. Now scientists will watch Dimorphos with everything from ground-based telescopes to deep-space observatories and see exactly how much of an effect DART's dramatic impact had on its target. "We're demonstrating for the first time that if humanity needed to alter the course of an asteroid, we would be capable of doing that," says Harrison Agrusa of the University of Maryland, a member of the DART team.

The DART mission was originally conceived some two decades ago, when scientists in the U.S. and Europe began to discuss a joint mission that could practice a kinetic asteroid deflection technique. Originally called AIDA (Asteroid Impact and Deflection Assessment), the mission would involve NASA's DART spacecraft and Europe's AIM (Asteroid Impact Mission) spacecraft, which would orbit the target and watch the impact. Sadly, European officials canceled AIM in 2016 because of a lack of funding. In 2019, however, the mission was reborn as the Hera spacecraft (named for the Greek goddess of marriage). But that reset in development meant a delayed launch: Hera won't lift off until 2024 and won't arrive at Didymos until 2026—much too late to witness DART's impact but still in time to study its enduring effects.

Scientists wanted DART's target to be a binary asteroid, where one asteroid orbits another, because such celestial configurations allow easier measurements of small, impact-induced orbital changes.

"The deflection is almost instantaneous," says Patrick Michel of the French National Center for Scientific Research, former lead scientist of AIM and now principal investigator of Hera. In 2013 scientists selected the Didymos system as the target. First found in 1996, that larger asteroid gained its name (Greek for "twin") following the discovery of a small orbiting companion in 2003, which was later dubbed Dimorphos, or "to have two forms."

Dimorphos completes an orbit of Didymos every 11.92 hours. The asteroids share a similar orbit with Earth yet pose no threat as they never come closer than a few million kilometers to our planet. But their angle of orbit means that Dimorphos regularly "eclipses" in front of Didymos, allowing its orbital period to be precisely measured. Following the impact, a variety of telescopes, including the James Webb Space Telescope and Hubble—and even spacecraft such as NASA's Lucy probe, which is currently on its way to visit asteroids near Jupiter—will track this eclipse, allowing scientists to work out just how much Dimorphos's orbit has been changed.

DART hit the asteroid nearly head on, meaning it slowed Dimorphos's orbit. The asteroid is so small, however, that mission scientists knew neither its exact shape nor its composition—whether Dimorphos was a rigid and solid object or rather a looser "rubble pile" of rocks and boulders that had gently accumulated together. During the final moments of its approach, DART beamed back images of Dimorphos's rubble-strewn surface, indicating the asteroid was far from rock-solid. If it had been, the change in its orbit could have been barely more than a minute because DART would have transferred only a relatively small amount of momentum to the asteroid. "We need at least 73 seconds of orbit change" for the mission to be heralded a success, Rivkin says.

Instead Dimorphos's shabby appearance suggests the force of outward-spewing material (perhaps as much as a few tens of millions of kilograms) could cause a much larger shift in momentum, shortening the asteroid's orbit by 10 minutes or more. Such an event could completely reshape Dimorphos or even send it tumbling head over heels. "The weaker the asteroid, the larger the crater," says Sabina

Raducan of the University of Bern in Switzerland, a DART team member. "Of course, we want there to be a lot of deflection and ejecta because that's more interesting."

Observations by telescopes and LICIACube should reveal roughly how much the orbit changed and how much ejecta was released, with the DART team set to announce preliminary results from the mission this December at a meeting of the American Geophysical Union in Chicago. But no one will know for certain how successful the mission was until Hera arrives in 2026. That spacecraft's observations will accurately measure the mass of Dimorphos and get a more exact sense of how much its orbit has changed around Didymos, perhaps 10 times better than would otherwise be possible from more remote observations alone. "We'll understand how big the push was and get a better understanding of what Dimorphos is made of," says Angela Stickle of APL, a DART team member.

That could be crucial information if something like DART is ever called on to save Earth in the future. "This is one of the most important things we're doing at the moment," says Detlef Koschny, deputy head of ESA's Planetary Defense Office. "We've been talking about the need to demonstrate that we can deflect an asteroid for many years." While no dinosaur-killer asteroids of several kilometers in size are known to be on an impact course with our planet, smaller asteroids like Dimorphos are less well constrained, with only an estimated few percent of their total population currently known. "We don't yet know enough to feel safe," Koschny says. An impact by a Dimorphos-sized space rock could instantly obliterate a city and cause widespread damage to an entire country, meaning there is good reason to look out for such asteroids.

Upcoming telescopes, such as the Vera C. Rubin Observatory, set to come online in Chile later this decade, will better track these asteroids. If we ever do find one on a collision course with Earth, the outcomes of the DART mission may well dictate what action we take. "It is going to validate a tool that we could use," Rivkin says. To divert a hazardous asteroid, perhaps a larger version of DART could be used or even a series of DART-sized spacecraft to slam into the offending space rock, one after another, incrementally deflecting its doom. "It depends on how much warning time we have," Rivkin says. Such a perilous event is unlikely to befall humanity anytime soon. But perhaps, far in the future, our distant descendants will have this little spacecraft to thank. "If we can deflect Dimorphos, we can most likely deflect any other near-Earth asteroid," Agrusa says.

About the Author

Jonathan O'Callaghan is an award-winning freelance journalist covering astronomy, astrophysics, commercial spaceflight and space exploration. Follow him on X (formerly Twitter) @Astro_Jonny.

NASA Asteroid Threat Practice Drill Shows We're Not Ready

By Matt Brady

On August 16, 2022, an approximately 70-meter asteroid entered Earth's atmosphere. At 2:02:10 p.m. EDT, the space rock exploded eight miles over Winston-Salem, N.C., with the energy of 10 megatons of TNT. The airburst virtually leveled the city and surrounding area. Casualties were in the thousands.

Well, not really. The destruction of Winston-Salem was the story line of the fourth Planetary Defense Tabletop Exercise, run by NASA's Planetary Defense Coordination Office. The exercise was a simulation where academics, scientists and government officials gathered to practice how the United States would respond to a real planet-threatening asteroid. It was held February 23 to 24, and participants were both virtual and in-person, hailing from Washington D.C., the Johns Hopkins Applied Physics Lab (APL) campus in Laurel, Md., Raleigh and Winston-Salem, N.C. The exercise included more than 200 participants from 16 different federal, state, and local organizations. On August 5, the final report came out, and the message was stark: humanity is not yet ready to meet this threat.

On the plus side, the exercise was meant to be hard—practically unwinnable. "We designed it to fall right into the gap in our capabilities," says Emma Rainey, an APL senior scientist who helped to create the simulation. "The participants could do nothing to prevent the impact." The main goal was testing the different government and scientific networks that should respond in a real-life planetary defense situation. "We want to see how effective operations and communications are between U.S. government agencies and the other organizations that would be involved, and then identify shortcomings," says Lindley Johnson, planetary defense officer at NASA headquarters.

All in all, the exercise demonstrated that the United States doesn't have the capability to intercept small, fast-moving asteroids, and our ability to see them is limited. Even if we could intercept space rocks, we may not be able to deflect one away from Earth, and using a nuclear weapon to destroy one is risky and filled with international legal issues. The trial also showed that misinformation—lies and false rumors spreading among the public—could drastically hamper the official effort. "Misinformation is not going away," says Angela Stickle, a senior research scientist at APL who helped design and facilitate the exercise. "We put it into the simulation because we wanted feedback on how to counteract it and take action if it was malicious."

Several key differences set this practice apart from previous ones in 2013, 2014, and 2016: First, this trial gave NASA's Planetary Defense Office a chance to stress-test the National Near-Earth Object Preparedness Strategy and Action Plan, released by the White House in 2018. The plan lays out the details of who does what and when within the federal government, which allowed this year's exercise to involve more governmental agencies than in previous years— including state and local emergency responders for the first time. The simulation was also the first to include not just an impact but its immediate aftereffects.

Events started with the "discovery" of an asteroid named "TTX22" heading toward Earth. Participants were presented with a crash course in asteroid science and told everything that was known about the asteroid and the likelihood of an impact. Each meeting jumped ahead in the timeline, with the final installments set just before and after the asteroid's impact near Winston-Salem.

The short but realistic timeline from discovery to impact highlighted major problems from the start. TTX22 was small and fast. By the time it was seen, it was too late to put together a mission to study, deflect or destroy it. NASA has no garages full of rockets on standby just in case an asteroid shows up. Shifting the rock's trajectory would require at least 12 kinetic impactors, each like NASA's DART mission that recently altered the orbit of the asteroid Dimorphos and which took more than five years to move from concept to rock-puncher. The recommendation from the after-action report on this front was blunt: develop these capabilities.

At the same time, the asteroid's velocity, unknown composition, and policy ramifications in the brief timeline ruled out hitting TTX22 with a nuclear bomb. However, late-in-the-game nuclear disruption remained an intriguing last-ditch option for some participants. "If you send up a nuclear explosive device, you could disrupt an asteroid just as it enters the atmosphere," Stickle says. "In theory."

That option, however, leans toward Hollywood, not reality. "There's this tendency to think, 'I saw this in a movie—they just launched ICBMs and blew it up,'" Johnson says. "The point of including this option in the simulation is to get them to understand that it's not as simple. Using a nuclear explosive device in the terminal phase of an impact is a situation we don't ever want to get ourselves into."

Blasting an asteroid in space may result in a cluster of smaller but still-dangerous, fast-moving rocks. And an upper-atmosphere detonation of a nuclear weapon has unknown but most likely dangerous effects. The explosion may not fully disintegrate the rock, forcing portions of it down somewhere else. Radiation could persist in the upper atmosphere at levels making traveling through it on your way to space prohibitive.

With no way to stop the asteroid from hitting Earth, the exercise was all about mitigation—what must be done leading up to the impact and in the immediate aftermath. Organizations at all levels needed to be in contact, emergency plans had to be developed and enacted, and the public informed.

Within the simulated timeline, misinformation was constant. Many online news stories about the asteroid were factually incorrect, while "asteroid deniers" and claims of "fake news" grew unabated. Misinformation was a regular source of frustration for participants, who recognized that they would need to address it head-on in a real-life situation.

Johnson explained that his office is attempting to play the long game against misinformation. "We want to establish NASA's Planetary Defense Coordination Office and those that work with us as the authorities when it comes to these situations," Johnson says. "The plan is that the media and public understand that a group at NASA tracks and manages these types of things."

But as participants pointed out, there are limited strategies to deal with a constant flow of lies from dozens or hundreds of outlets in a short time frame. In this case, misinformation yielded a deadly toll. "When we discussed evacuation, we were told that 20 percent of people would not leave because it was all fake news or the government was lying or some other reason," says August Vernon, Winston-Salem/Forsyth County emergency management director. "That was about 200,000 people, all spread out. So here I am, not sure we'd even be able to evacuate the hospitals and prisons, and then we have people that can leave, refusing to leave."

The news had a somber effect on the participants as they waited for the revelations of the simulation's final "day," August 16. After academic participants explained the energy release the region would experience, Vernon was blunt. "There would be collapsed buildings," he says, "we'd lose our hospitals, a lot of our infrastructure would be gone, there was a chance this could take out cell phone reception for at least 50 miles, and the whole region would lose power."

The simulation presented a final misinformation gut punch. Post-impact, an individual calling themselves "National Expert T.X. Asteroid" claimed the explosion released toxic materials from outer space into the atmosphere. As a result, residents should expect symptoms similar to radiation exposure. The baseless claims were all over social media, and "T.X" was giving interviews to news outlets.

On the positive side, NASA's ability to disseminate information received high marks from participants, given the agency's widespread credibility. In addition, the framework established in the White House plan also appeared robust enough to manage the flow of information between federal and state agencies and activate all necessary communication channels.

The conversations between federal and local officials provided some of the best results of the exercise: decision-makers at all levels reached new understandings regarding who would coordinate the post-impact rescue and recovery efforts and what they needed to do their jobs. One finding was that sometimes at the fine-grain levels, less is more in terms of communicating the science. "We couldn't keep up sometimes, and that's something they need to consider," Vernon says. "I have mayors, fire chiefs, and other folks to explain this to. We may not need to know all the science behind it, but we need to know what, when and where because we need to start making big decisions as early as possible."

Participants also discovered that the face of the "expert" should change from the federal to the local level. "At our level, we asked who our lead spokesperson would be," Vernon says. "Who would people respect, trust, and believe when we find out it's headed towards us? That might not be the same person NASA puts out there."

Ultimately, the participants and the simulation's facilitators agreed that the biggest thing they lacked was time. The asteroid destroyed Winton-Salem because of the narrow window between its discovery and impact. Widening that window is critical. "A decade is a fairly comfortable timeframe to be able to do something that would be effective," Stickle says. "Thirty years would be ideal. That's enough time for detailed observations, planning, building a spacecraft and getting something big to move. You'd even have time to send up a replacement if something goes wrong."

There are promising signs that with enough warning, humanity could mount a successful response. The DART mission, for instance, already showed that a spacecraft's impact can alter a space rock's trajectory. Multiple surveys of near-Earth objects, asteroids and comets are ongoing, and NASA received $55 million more for planetary defense from Congress than it asked for.

"It's going to take time and money to detect and characterize everything out there," Rainey says. "As well as having the ability for missions that can get underway rapidly and be effective against something like this. But ultimately, that's much cheaper than rebuilding a city." But just in case, Vernon says, "At least now, we have a plan. Hopefully, it never has to be used."

About the Author

Matt Brady is a high school science teacher and author of The Science of Rick and Morty. *His interests focus on the intersection of pop culture and science.*

Section 5: Climate Change and Eco-Collapse

There's Still Time to Fix Climate—About 11 Years

By Mark Fischetti

On October 31 world leaders will descend on Glasgow, Scotland, for the United Nations Climate Change Conference, or COP26, in a last-ditch effort to defuse the climate emergency by limiting global warming to less than 1.5 degrees Celsius. Reaching that level would still bring violent storms, deep flooding, gripping droughts, and problematic sea-level rise, but it would avert even more severe consequences. Global temperature has risen by nearly 1.1 degrees C since the Industrial Revolution.

A clear understanding of how emissions affect temperature shows that there is still time to reach the political agreements, economic transformations, and public buy-in needed to sharply cut emissions, limit temperature rise and limit destruction. Nations can duck the 1.5-degree ceiling if they make deep cuts now. As of July 30, commitments to reduce emissions by the 191 nations that signed the 2015 Paris Climate Accord would permit 2.7 degrees of warming by 2100, according to a report issued in September by the secretariat of the U.N. Framework Convention on Climate Change, the group that coordinates ongoing pledges to the Paris Accord. The charge for the COP26 meeting is to eliminate the gap. Here's what needs to happen.

The first step is to get rid of an old idea that the public, the media, and policymakers are not clear on—the notion that even if humans stopped emitting carbon dioxide overnight, inertia in the climate system would continue to raise temperature for many years. Because CO_2 can persist in the atmosphere for a century or more, the argument goes, even if the concentration stopped rising, temperature would keep going up because the heat-trapping mechanism is already in place. In other words, some level of future warming is "baked into" the system, so it's too late to avoid the 1.5-degree threshold.

But scientists discounted that idea at least a decade ago. Climate models consistently show that "committed" (baked-in) warming does not happen. As soon as CO_2 emissions stop rising, the atmospheric concentration of CO_2 levels off and starts to slowly fall because the oceans, soils and vegetation keep absorbing CO_2, as they always do. Temperature doesn't rise further. It also doesn't drop, because atmospheric and ocean interactions adjust and balance out. The net effect is that "temperature does not go up or down," says Joeri Rogelj, director of research at the Grantham Institute–Climate Change and Environment at Imperial College London. The good news is that if nations can cut emissions substantially and quickly, warming can be held to less than 1.5 degrees.

To avoid that threshold, the world can emit only a set amount of CO_2 from now into the future. This quantity is known as the carbon budget. In 2019, the year before the COVID pandemic depressed the global economy, the world discharged about 42 gigatons of CO_2–similar to the 2018 level and to what is happening in 2021. According to the midrange scenario in the Intergovernmental Panel on Climate Change's comprehensive report released in August, "Climate Change 2021: The Physical Science Basis," another 500 gigatons of CO_2 emissions will raise global temperature by 1.5 degrees. Nations have about 11 more years at current emissions rates—2032—before exhausting the budget.

That threshold moves further into the future, however, if countries significantly reduce their output very soon. Aggressive policies, enacted now, can create more time and more hope for preventing catastrophe. In a 2018 report, the IPCC stated that the world had to achieve net-zero carbon emissions by 2050 to keep warming to 1.5 degrees. To get on that track, the September UN report says, nations have to cut emissions in half by 2030. Every year of delay brings the world much closer to the edge of the precipice. "We are not trying to hit the temperature targets," says Rogelj, who is also a senior research scholar at the International Institute for Applied Systems Analysis and a key author of the 2021 IPCC report. "We are trying to stay as far away from the edge as possible."

Degrees of Risk

If nations fall short and the temperature rise surpasses 1.5 degrees, it will still be crucial to make immediate and ongoing reductions to stay below 2.0 degrees of warming, a level at which scientists say impacts become more dire and exceedingly difficult for societies to cope with. To avoid that threshold, the world can emit only another 1,350 gigatons of CO_2, according to the August IPCC report. At 42 gigatons a year, that happens by 2052. Again, if countries greatly reduce emissions soon, that date extends forward, too.

If countries do not make significant reductions this decade, the subsequent cuts needed to limit temperature rise to 2.0 degrees will be much tougher to achieve. "Every single year that passes imposes a huge penalty for the future reductions that would be required," says Josep Canadell, chief research scientist at CSIRO, Australia's national science agency, and a lead author of the 2021 IPCC report.

It is also important to understand, Rogelj says, that each added 10th of a degree of warming beyond 1.5 degrees brings greater risk of damaging weather, sea-level rise and other ills to more ecosystems and more people, especially the most vulnerable. He likens the increasing risk to jumping from a platform that today may be a meter high: healthy adults might hit the ground without injury, but small children and the elderly will get hurt. Each additional 10th of a degree raises the platform. "At two meters," Rogelj says, "many more people are likely to get injured. And at a certain height, everyone will be severely harmed."

The IPCC's carbon budget analysis includes a measure of uncertainty—roughly 15 percent up or down. And the midrange scenario means nations have a 50 percent chance of keeping warming to 1.5 degrees if they restrict future emissions to 500 gigatons. To improve the odds to 83 percent, the IPCC says, the budget drops to 300 gigatons. The numbers get even tighter if nations continue to burn down rain forests because there will be less vegetation drawing CO_2 from the atmosphere. Countries have to consider societal factors as well, such as being sure to spread any economic challenges from emissions cuts fairly on citizens.

Of course, if the world reduced emissions only marginally and never reaches net zero, "atmospheric CO_2 concentration will continue to increase, and temperature will continue to rise," says Susan Solomon, a professor of environmental studies and atmospheric chemistry at the Massachusetts Institute of Technology, who has contributed to many climate change reports.

Human Lag

The dialogue leading up to COP26, where countries will try to encourage one another to commit to greater emissions reductions, is focused on CO_2. But the atmosphere is affected by other greenhouse gases such as methane and nitrous oxide, by climate feedbacks such as disappearing sea ice, and by aerosols—small pollution particles released primarily from the burning of fossil fuels. If CO_2 emissions remain at current levels, but methane emissions rise and other feedbacks get stronger, the world will warm by 1.5 degrees before 2032 and by 2.0 degrees before 2052. The IPCC scenarios include some level of additional warming from these factors. They do not include any so-called negative emissions by machines that pull CO_2 from the sky, because the economic viability of those systems is just too uncertain, Canadell says.

The U.N. report uses a different metric to account for other greenhouse gases, called CO_2-equivalent—a quantity that represents warming from CO_2 as well as methane, nitrous oxides and other gases such as hydrofluorocarbons. But its analyses parallel the IPCC's. As of July 30, the U.N. report says, 113 of the 191 nations that signed the Paris Accord had made some level of commitment to reduce emissions. Under the latest promises, global emissions by 2030 would actually be 5.0 percent higher than in 2019—not lower—in the midrange scenario the IPCC uses. The report notes that emissions from the nations that have issued revised goals since 2015, as a group, would indeed be lower in 2030 compared with 2019, so the net increase worldwide would come from the countries that have not improved their original commitments and countries that have never committed.

At current emissions rates, the U.N. report says, the world would use up 89 percent of the remaining 1.5-degree budget by 2030 and 39 percent of the 2.0-degree budget by 2030. On October 25, a week before COP26 begins, the secretariat was to count any additional country updates made since July 30. Eyes will be on the G20 nations—19 nations plus the European Union that together account for about 90 percent of gross world product. The G20 nations are responsible for about three quarters of global emissions, according to Taryn Fransen, a senior fellow at the World Resources Institute who studies nations' long-term climate strategies. She is eager to hear how countries will fulfill their promises, known as nationally determined contributions, or NDCs. The net-zero goals are important, Fransen says, "but each country has to actually get there."

To get there, nations have to jump—now. Some scientists are starting to use the old climate change language to highlight what has to be done. The warming factor that is baked in "is human infrastructure," Solomon says. If countries let the current stocks of coal plants, natural gas facilities, transportation systems, industrial complexes, and buildings live out their natural lifetimes, they commit to a certain amount of additional warming. There is also a lag time in stopping temperature rise, she notes, "a lag in human action—the slow response of people to the problem." The practical question, says Raymond Pierrehumbert, head of the Planetary Climate Dynamics Group at the University of Oxford, is: How quickly can the world scrub greenhouse gases out of the global economy?

About the Author

Mark Fischetti has been a senior editor at Scientific American *for 17 years and has covered sustainability issues, including climate, weather, environment, energy, food, water, biodiversity, population, and more. He assigns and edits feature articles, commentaries and news by journalists and scientists and also writes in those formats. He edits History, the magazine's department looking at science advances throughout time. He was founding managing editor of two spinoff magazines:* Scientific American Mind *and* Scientific American Earth 3.0. *His 2001 freelance article for the magazine, "Drowning New Orleans," predicted the widespread disaster that a storm like Hurricane Katrina would impose on the city. His video* What Happens to Your Body after You Die? *has more than 12 million views on YouTube. Fischetti has written freelance articles for the* New York Times, Sports Illustrated, Smithsonian, Technology Review, Fast Company, *and many others. He co-authored the book* Weaving the Web *with Tim Berners-Lee, inventor of the World Wide Web, which tells the real story of how the Web was created. He also co-authored* The New Killer Diseases *with microbiologist Elinor Levy. Fischetti is a former managing editor of* IEEE Spectrum Magazine *and of* Family Business Magazine. *He has a physics degree and has twice served as the Attaway Fellow in Civic Culture at Centenary College of Louisiana, which awarded him an honorary doctorate. In 2021 he received the American Geophysical Union's Robert C. Cowen Award for Sustained Achievement in Science Journalism, which celebrates a career of outstanding reporting on the Earth and space sciences. He has appeared on NBC's Meet the Press, CNN, the History Channel, NPR News and many news radio stations. Follow Fischetti on X (formerly Twitter) @markfischetti.*

Extreme Heat Is Deadlier Than Hurricanes, Floods, and Tornadoes Combined

By Terri Adams-Fuller

On June 25, 2022, Esteban Chavez Jr. started his day like any other, working his route in Pasadena, Calif., as a driver for UPS. But the city was in the middle of an intense heat wave, and by midafternoon the temperature was higher than 90 degrees Fahrenheit. After completing his last delivery of the day, Chavez collapsed off his seat in the cab of the truck. He went unnoticed for 20 minutes before the homeowner at his delivery location saw him and sought medical assistance. Chavez's family said he died from heatstroke as a result of heat exhaustion. He was 24 years old.

Chavez didn't seem like someone at risk for the health effects of extreme heat. But such unfortunate deaths are increasingly common. The number of heat-related illnesses and fatalities in the U.S. has been going up since the 1980s—a direct result of the rise in Earth's temperatures. Approximately 1,300 people die in the U.S. every year from exposure to extreme heat, according to the Environmental Protection Agency, and that figure that will almost certainly increase with the accelerating effects of climate change. This phenomenon is, of course, not exclusive to the U.S.; a study published in 2021 by the *Lancet* reports that 356,000 people in nine countries—about half the population of Vermont—died from illnesses related to extreme heat in 2019.

Exposure to extreme heat can damage the central nervous system, the brain, and other vital organs, and the effects can set in with terrifying speed, resulting in heat exhaustion, heat cramps, or heatstroke. It also exacerbates existing medical conditions such as hypertension and heart disease and is especially perilous for people who suffer from chronic diseases. The older population is at high risk, and children, who may not be able to regulate their body temperatures as effectively as adults in extreme conditions, are also vulnerable. But people of all ages can be endangered. Studies show that outdoor workers regardless of age are most likely to experience the consequences of extreme heat exposure.

Extreme heat is the number-one weather-related cause of death in the U.S., and it kills more people most years than hurricanes, floods, and tornadoes combined. Yet research shows that compared with their thinking about dramatic events such as storm surges and wildfires, people tend to feel more uncertain about what to do under the threat of extreme heat and don't perceive as much personal risk. This mismatch between the reality of the danger and the actions people take to protect themselves extends beyond individual perception to the policy level. Heat risks to human health are not often prioritized in climate mitigation and adaptation plans—if they are factored in at all.

Discriminatory Policies and Urban Hotspots

Between 1880, when precise recordkeeping began, and 1980, average temperatures worldwide rose by about 0.13 degree F every 10 years. Since 1981 the rate of increase has more than doubled, and for the past 40 years global annual temperatures have increased by 0.32 degree F per decade. Although the pace of the increase might seem relatively slow, it signals a dramatic shift, and the cumulative effects on the planet are huge. The 10 hottest years on record have occurred since 2010. The summer of 2022 was the hottest in known history for segments of the U.S. Temperatures soared to 127 degrees F in Death Valley, Calif., where extremes are expected. But record highs were also reached across the U.S. in cities that aren't accustomed to severe heat, such as Bonners Ferry, Idaho (108 degrees F), and Omak, Wash. (117 degrees F).

Extreme heat is a danger to all segments of society, but people in dense urban environments suffer the most severely. The connection between urbanization and heat risks will become more urgent as more people around the world move to urban areas. According to the United Nations Population Division, 68 percent of the planet's population will live in urban areas by 2050, up from 55 percent in 2018. The rate of global urbanization, however, hides differences across nations: 82 percent of people in North America already live in urban environments compared with 65 percent in China and 43 percent in Africa. In the U.S., the rate of urbanization (people moving from rural areas to cities) increased from 50 percent in the 1950s to 83 percent in 2020. This rapid growth on top of environmental changes compounds stressors on human health, infrastructure, socioeconomic systems, and essential resources such as energy and water.

Urban centers tend to have a high density of buildings, paved roads and parking lots—all of which absorb and retain heat. Green spaces such as parks and golf courses, in contrast, reduce heat levels in neighborhoods by lowering surface and air temperatures through evapotranspiration. Mature trees and other natural features provide shade, deflect the sun's radiation and release moisture into the atmosphere. As heat waves become more frequent and intense, cities are experiencing higher nighttime and mean temperatures compared with areas that have a lot of green space. This is commonly called the heat island effect.

Within these heat islands are especially hot hotspots, or intraurban heat islands, which tend to have the least green space. Recent studies have shown that "extreme heat exposure is highly unequal and severely impacts the urban poor," as stated in a 2021 paper in the *Proceedings of the National Academy of Sciences USA*. The link between vulnerable populations and the lack of green space in the neighborhoods where they live results from cascading issues; among them are policies designed to restrict the upward mobility of certain groups, such as redlining practices that date back to the 1930s.

The term "redlining" denotes the assignment of grades to residential areas based on their racial composition; the lower-graded neighborhoods were less likely to receive investments, and people living in them had a harder time obtaining loans. The redlining practice grew from President Franklin D. Roosevelt's federally funded New Deal, which enforced segregation practices. The Federal Housing Administration, for instance, refused to insure the homes of Black and other nonwhite families or homes owned by white people that were considered too close to Black neighborhoods. Local governments that practiced "benign neglect" created isolated zones devoid of resources and opportunities.

Today's hotspot communities often suffer from the long-term effects of these discriminatory urban-planning policies, including inadequate access to parks and green spaces. And for people who live in these areas, central air-conditioning may not be an affordable solution, if it's even an available option. Many older buildings have never been retrofitted to accommodate central air—a common situation in the inner city in places such as New York, Detroit, and Baltimore—leaving people reliant on smaller, portable window units and fans.

Regardless of the cooling technology used, low-income households in America spend 8.1 percent of their income on energy costs compared with 2.3 percent for non-low-income households, according to a 2020 report from the American Council for an Energy Efficient Economy. The ability to reduce energy costs (by updating house insulation and switching to efficient electric appliances, for instance) is largely out of the control of renters and may be unaffordable for lower-income homeowners. Thus, the most vulnerable people in the hottest hot zones must face decisions that pit the high energy cost of staying cool and safe against providing for other necessities of life. As a result, they may be more at risk for heat-related illness and death because of both overexposure to high temperatures where they live and the lack of resources to mitigate the effects of that heat.

Better Risk Assessment

In the past the heat island effect had little connection to global climate trends, but recent research findings suggest that, on average, urban heat island warming will be equivalent to about half the warming caused by greenhouse gas emissions by the year 2050. In other words, cities get a double punch: both climate change and urban development that swaps green space for pavement are warming metropolitan areas, influencing the chemistry of the atmosphere and intensifying urban air pollution. Currently global temperatures are predicted to increase by 3.8 to 6.3 degrees F by 2100—resulting in intolerable heat thresholds for urban environments.

Given the scope of the problem, how can we lessen the negative effects of extreme heat events on historically vulnerable urban communities? At Howard University's NOAA Cooperative Science Center for Atmospheric Sciences and Meteorology, my colleagues and I are interested in understanding how people process risk associated with extreme heat and respond to heat advisories. As scholars from disciplines spanning atmospheric sciences, communications, computer science, and sociology, we want to learn how to inform better decision-making in communities so we can help them make useful and realistic plans for both the short and the long term.

Our current work is taking place in Baltimore, which ranks among the U.S. cities with the most intense urban heat island effects. A 2020 study led by Jeremy Hoffman of the Center for Environmental Studies at Virginia Commonwealth University showed that in Baltimore neighborhoods where a history of redlining practices has blocked investment, summer temperatures are nearly six degrees F hotter than the citywide average. The research project uses an integrative citizen science approach, giving us an excellent opportunity to learn from members of communities experiencing some of the worst effects. To assess people's responses to weather forecasts and heat events in Baltimore, we developed an app that merges weather data, risk communication and behavioral health information to push messages to study participants. The app also collects behavioral responses to extreme heat alerts.

Some early research activities involved talking with city residents to discern how they perceive and respond to extreme heat events. As part of this, we asked about their awareness of warnings and potential impacts of exposure. We conducted interaction-based interviews with focus groups, which allowed us to observe conversations among participants and hear both individual and collective responses.

When asked about their level of awareness concerning heat advisories, many focus group participants appeared to have general knowledge about the topic: they reported being aware of heat advisory warnings, and the majority said they modified their behavior in response to those warnings by trying to drink more water and delaying physical activities until later in the day. Most people, however, were unsure of the meanings behind the different threat levels, which are typically presented as part of a weather forecast, and were confused about how to interpret them. For instance, some people were not aware of the difference between a heat "watch" (be prepared) and a heat "warning" (take action now to protect yourself).

We also found that people have very limited knowledge of the "heat index"—a measure that factors in relative humidity to estimate how a given day's temperature actually feels to the human body. This data point is superior to temperature alone for alerting the public to especially dangerous types of heat. It became clear to us that people would additionally benefit from greater awareness of the effects of climate change in general, so they would know to expect heat-related problems to get worse over time.

One of our essential findings is that knowledge of general heat risks does not necessarily lead to an accurate perception of one's own risk. Several study participants indicated that they were aware of the different ways people could protect themselves from heat, but this knowledge did not translate into their *personally* taking protective actions. Some participants said they do not believe they are at direct risk. As one person put it: "To me, it being 90 degrees did not really say anything [because I'm] from the Caribbean. Like, sometimes it is 100, 105." Interestingly, our study's older participants, considered by health professionals as high risk for the dangerous effects of heat exposure, did not think of themselves as especially at risk.

This summer the Howard University team is distributing air monitors, internet hotspots, and cell phones (for those who do not currently own one) to community members who elected to participate in the study. These tools will collect data at no cost to the participants, who will receive $200 for taking part in the project over three months. The real-time indoor weather data will enable us to monitor heat exposure. As temperatures rise, the study participants will be alerted to the onset of an extreme heat event or heat wave via an app or, when appropriate, phone calls and email. They will be reminded to use the app to access information on the heat index, as well as the risk of extreme heat exposure and suggested protective actions. The types of help and resources recommended by the app will be personalized for the study participants based on their individual risk factors.

Subsequent alerts will be tailored to the needs of the target population, with particular attention to message framing. This approach will include a clear and easy-to-digest explanation of the levels of risk uncertainty to help people understand why they should take action even if some parts of the forecast don't come to fruition. We think people need more information to best manage their expectations, not just to make good decisions. It's important for them to do so because the National Weather Service is increasingly incorporating the language and visuals of uncertainty into public discussions that reflect the estimates in forecast models. After data have been collected, study participants will be surveyed for insights on how the messaging influenced their self-protective actions and help-seeking behaviors.

Although there is no fail-safe approach to addressing the risks associated with high heat exposure, talking more about what's at stake is a good start. The potential dangers of excessive heat extend beyond physiological health to facets of life such as increased rates of domestic violence and crime. There are economic consequences, too: according to the Atlantic Council, the U.S. could lose some $100 billion annually because of extreme heat effects.

The hope is that increased awareness of the gap between risk and protective actions will force policy makers to take these issues more seriously and factor them into climate-preparedness plans. Opening cooling centers during a heat wave might not be enough to prevent unnecessary deaths if people don't think they need to go. More effective communication is one critical tool for reducing the harmful consequences of extreme heat on human health.

About the Author

Terri Adams-Fuller is a professor in the department of sociology and criminology and interim director at the NOAA Cooperative Science Center for Atmospheric Sciences and Meteorology at Howard University. Her research interests include emergency management, policing, gender studies, and how disasters affect people and organizations.

Carbon in the Oceans Is Altering the Micro-Fabric of Life

By David Ewing Duncan

When the waters south of Miami turned Jacuzzi hot this summer, topping out at 101.1 degrees Fahrenheit in Manatee Bay, scientists agonized over the impact on parrotfish, grunts, spiny lobsters, and coral reefs. But what about the invisible world of the ocean's microbiome that we can't see—one of bacteria, fungi, algae, and viruses?

Before you say "ewww," you should know that these tiny creatures, which on Earth number more than stars in the universe, connect all life on our planet. Scientists have found them deep in ocean chasms, and in volcanic vents, glaciers, caves, and mines. They provide most of the oxygen in the atmosphere and help organisms digest food and manage immune systems. When creatures—including people—die, microbes decompose them, releasing carbon, nitrogen, and phosphates that create new life. Roughly 38 trillion bacteria live inside and on you right now. Without bacteria and all that they do, you wouldn't stay alive very long.

Nor will humans fare well on a planet where our indiscriminate use of fossil fuels and industrial chemicals continues to alter the delicate balance of microbes that sustain our ecosystem, into one that does not. Billions of years of evolution have shifted the Earth from a carbon-rich atmosphere to one drenched in oxygen. Over those eons, microbes mostly accomplished this terraforming by feeding on carbon and producing the oxygen we breathe as a byproduct, a process that humans seem hell-bent on reversing unless we act quickly to preserve the world of the very small by radically reducing carbon emissions and the indiscriminate use of other chemicals.

Humans are subjecting the Earth's microbiome to the equivalent of what happens when you eat fast-food burgers and potato chips 24/7. You get a bellyache, or worse, in part because processed foods and high fructose corn syrup alter the composition of bacteria in our gut, decreasing the influence of "good" bacteria and increasing "bad" bacteria. Likewise, carbon and other pollutants alter the microbiome of Earth and undermine planetwide ecological systems that most people are only vaguely aware of.

For example, tiny ocean microbes called phytoplankton not only produce much of the oxygen on Earth, but also sequester almost 30 percent of the carbon produced by humans each year. Called the marine biological carbon pump, or just the biological pump, the system that supports phytoplankton is increasingly under threat as sea temperatures rise and phytoplankton drown in carbon. "We're lucky we have the oceans to sponge up so much CO_2," says Chris Dupont, an oceanographer and microbiologist at the J. Craig Venter Institute in La Jolla, Calif. "If the pump that drives this ever stopped working, we'd be in big trouble."

Rising levels of CO_2 make seawater more acidic. This harms microbes sensitive to changes in pH. Pollution from phosphates and nitrogen from fertilizers on land are flowing from rivers into oceans and causing dead zones where the water is hypoxic, containing less than two parts per million of oxygen, an environment where few (or no) fish or other marine life can survive. A dead zone below the mouth of the Mississippi River in the Gulf of Mexico has reached the size of New Jersey and, while it fluctuates in size according to the season and from year to year, overall it has been growing bigger. Globally, the number of dead zones has doubled every decade since the 1960s and now number in the hundreds, occurring from the Baltic Sea to the coasts of Latin America and Africa and the Great Lakes. The largest dead zone in the world is a 63,700-square-mile swath of the Gulf of Oman, almost the size of Florida.

Warming oceans and out-of-control chemical use cause coral reefs to eject bacteria and tiny algae called zooxanthellae that live in their tissue and provide them with important nutrients. Zooxanthellae help remove waste and fend off pathogens and are responsible for coral's vibrant colors. Their loss contributes to reefs' dyeing, bleached white. More heat in the North Atlantic also spurs rising levels of a toxic bacteria species called *Vibrio*, which causes intestinal illnesses, including cholera, in humans, according to a 2016 study. *Vibrio vulnificus*, the so-called flesh-eating bacteria, and *Karenia brevis*, a toxic algae species that can kill fish and cause respiratory and other problems in manatees, sea turtles and humans, are among other nasty pathogens on the rise along parts of the North Atlantic coast. These microbes are often associated with "red tides" that are increasingly inundating the coasts of Florida and other shores as algae thrive in warmer waters and gorge on nutrients in fertilizer runoff.

Scientists can only guess what hot-tub level temperatures off Florida are doing to microbes living there. "One-hundred-degree Fahrenheit water will obviously change the microbiome, but in truth we do not know the ramifications," marine biologist Jack Gilbert of the University of California, San Diego, told me. "Microbes are highly adaptable, but as these changes become more routine, we will see a shift in community dynamics and their metabolic activity that could have ramifications throughout the food chain."

As the world moves to limit human activity contributing to climate change, it's critical that the effect on Earth's smallest creatures be considered alongside concerns for more photo-friendly species like Adélie penguins, wild tulips, piper plovers—and the aforementioned parrotfish and spiny lobsters. That's a point made in a new book, *The Voyage of the Sorcerer II:Explorations into the Microbiome of the Oceans*, which I co-authored with geneticist Craig Venter. The book describes his two decades of work scouring the world's oceans for microbes from a 100-foot sailboat.

"It's hard to get the attention of politicians and others about what's happening," says Dupont. But scientists are trying. For instance, in 2019, a group of 34 microbiologists published a paper titled "Scientists' Warning to Humanity: Microorganisms and Climate Change." The authors put "humanity on notice that the impact of climate change will depend heavily on responses of microorganisms, which are essential for achieving an environmentally sustainable future."

As we think small about climate change it becomes clear that nature is responding to the ongoing chemical assault by "striking back in unexpected ways"—a warning delivered in 1962 when marine biologist Rachel Carson wrote *Silent Spring*. Six decades later we're seeing what she meant with superhot oceans, heat domes, raging fires, floods, crop losses, and superstorms. Now we can add that nature is striking back through Earth's smallest creatures, as humanity shifts the microscopic life that sustains us to a planet that, more and more, does not.

This is an opinion and analysis article, and the views expressed by the author or authors are not necessarily those of Scientific American.

About the Author

David Ewing Duncan is the co-author with J. Craig Venter of The Voyage of Sorcerer II: Explorations into the Microbiome of the Oceans *(Harvard University Press).*

Our Fragile Earth: How Close Are We to Climate Catastrophe?

By Mark Fischetti

N o one can predict the future. But sometimes we can get a solid idea of what's coming by looking at the past. In his new book, *Our Fragile Moment: How Lessons from Earth's Past Can Help Us Survive the Climate Crisis*, renowned climate scientist Michael Mann describes the world climate change is creating based on what we know from specific times in Earth's four-billion-year history when the planet was extremely hot or extremely cold.

Scientific American asked Mann, director of the Penn Center for Science, Sustainability and the Media at the University of Pennsylvania, to give us the main lessons from each era and to explain the warning, and the hope, they provide for today and the future. As Mann says in his book's intro, "the collective evidence from ... the paleoclimate record of Earth's past climatic changes ... actually provides a blueprint for what we need to do to preserve our fragile moment" on a planet that has survived much more than what we humans could.

[An edited transcript of the interview follows.]

Q: Let's start with the first two eras: the Faint Young Sun era was three billion years ago, and then Snowball Earth occurred 800 to 550 million years ago. What happened, and what did we learn?

A: Early on, the sun was 30 percent less bright, but the planet wasn't frozen; the oceans were teeming with life already. As the sun gradually got brighter and brighter, the concentration of carbon dioxide in the atmosphere got lower and lower during a couple billion years. As living organisms spread, they moderated the atmosphere and temperature. It suggests that there are restorative mechanisms—that life itself helps keep the planet within livable bounds. But only to a point!

Cyanobacteria loaded Earth's atmosphere with oxygen, which had previously been largely anoxic [deficient in oxygen]. Oxygen scavenges methane, so there was a rapid disappearance of methane; Earth lost that early methane greenhouse effect. Positive feedback loops occurred. The planet spun out of control into a snowball.

Life can help keep the planet within habitable bounds, but it can also push the planet beyond those boundaries. Today we are the living things that are impacting our climate. Is our future one of resilience or instability? The paleoclimate record tells us we're somewhere in between. We can still achieve stability, but if we continue burning fossil fuels, we will have instability.

Q: **A massive buildup of carbon dioxide in the atmosphere 250 million years ago, during the Permian period, led to the Great Dying, when most life on Earth was wiped out. What does it tell us about the so-called sixth extinction we're in right now?**

A: The Permian has the greatest documented extinction—something like 90 percent of all life went extinct. There was great natural warming driven by unusually active volcanism that loaded the atmosphere with carbon dioxide. It warmed the planet rapidly on a geological timescale, although it was nowhere near the rapidity of what we're doing today.

Some people cite this era as a reason for believing that we are experiencing runaway warming and that our extinction is now ensured. They say we're experiencing runaway methane-driven warming from thawing permafrost—and that it's too late to do anything about it; we'll all be extinct. But I spent quite a bit of time going through the literature, and it doesn't hold up. There's no evidence that there was any major release of methane at that time. There are a whole bunch of things that make it a bad analogue for today. I go through them in the book. For example, there was a massive continent that was very dry with very tenuous, early forests that were very vulnerable to wildfire and to collapse. So there was a much greater potential for massive deforestation and therefore a massive lowering of oxygen. There was also a huge increase in sulfur in the ocean that probably extinguished quite a bit of sea life.

There are all these things that contributed to that particular catastrophe that aren't analogous today. There's no evidence that we're going to see substantial lowering of oxygen concentrations from anything that we're doing. There's no evidence that we're seeing massive releases of sulfur—although deoxygenation like the Black Sea has experienced, with a larger anoxic zone and die-offs, is a bit of a warning.

Q: About 56 million years ago Earth became very hot again—as hot as it ever has been. This was the so-called Paleocene-Eocene Thermal Maximum, the PETM. Are we headed for that instead?

A: This is the same as the Great Dying. Scientists no longer think that methane played a major role in the PETM. But there is a different lesson. The PETM is notable for the rapid warmup—it happened not across millions of years but in as short as 10,000 or 20,000 years. This is very rapid from a geological standpoint, although, again, it's 100 times slower than today. The warming spike happened on top of an already warm planet; it took the planet to temperatures higher than anything that's documented in the geological record.

The PETM reached levels of heat that would be dangerous for human beings, and we are already encountering wet-bulb temperatures [an estimation of the effect of temperature and humidity] that are deadly in some parts of the world. The PETM would have been a world where large parts of the planet were too hot for humans. So people say, "Oh, look, life adapted." There was a massive miniaturization of some species. Horses shrunk 30 percent in order to adapt [smaller bodies, with a higher ratio of surface area to volume, have less trouble shedding heat]. The reality is that when you see something so dramatic as horses shrinking by 30 percent, that means there would have been very large amounts of maladaptive species; there would be a massive loss of life along the way. The idea is that human beings can just adapt, but those selective pressures don't favor anyone.

Q: Let's jump back 10 million years before the PETM to 65 million years ago. An enormous asteroid struck Earth, shrouding the planet in dust, which rapidly cooled its surface, killing the land-based dinosaurs (not the avian ones). That's very different from earlier events and from climate change today. What can that episode tell us?

A: The dust very rapidly cooled the planet, so any animal that couldn't burrow into the ground or find shelter—everything larger than a dog, basically—died out. The climate story is that even though it's a scenario of global cooling rather than global warming, it was rapid. [The event is also known as the K–Pg boundary, the transition between the Cretaceous period and the Paleogene period.]

This also relates to societal fragility. In the height of the cold war, we were focused on nuclear winter. An all-out nuclear war would shroud the planet with dust, smoke, and ash. The fate that befell the dinosaurs could be our fate. Carl Sagan, of course, was the one who really raised awareness. He and his colleagues published a paper in late 1983 that said it isn't just the physical destruction that'll get us; what will really get us is the rapid cooling of the planet.

As the cold war ended, the world felt that that particular threat had waned. But with recent tensions with Russia's invasion of Ukraine and the threat by Putin to use tactical nuclear weapons, all of a sudden this threat has reemerged. The point that applies from the dinosaurs is that it isn't the absolute levels of warmth that matter today; it's the planet we are evolved for. The dinosaurs had evolved for a certain climate, and when it cooled rapidly, they perished. Other animals were able to exploit the niches that emerged. Ironically, it was our ancestors, the early mammals. In one sense, we're here because the dinosaurs perished. If we have

8 billion people adapted to a climate that is disappearing as we continue to warm the planet, that's a real danger.

Q: **Much more recently we've had several ice ages; the Last Glacial Maximum was about 20,000 years ago. What did these cold periods reveal about our increasingly hot period now?**

A: The K–Pg event was a punctuated interval of cooling during an otherwise warm era. About three million years ago, CO2 levels dropped to near what they are today. To some extent, the Pleistocene [which started about 2.6 million years ago] is a better analogue for our climate today. There was no Greenland ice sheet. Sea levels were 10 feet higher at least, maybe 20. The planet was warmer than it is today. Is that the future that we are now committed to? The answer isn't so clear-cut because of hysteresis [when a physical change lags the force that created it]. The behavior of things when you're on a cooling scenario is different from the behavior of things when you're on a warming scenario. You can reach the same point, and the climate can look very different depending on how you got there. It's probably not the case that we have committed yet to the melting the Greenland ice sheet. That hysteresis effect buys us a little bit of a margin of error but not a big one. Maybe it buys us a half a degree more warming. Once again it shows us the fragile nature of this moment. We could soon exceed that range of resilience if we continue on the path we're on.

Q: **The last timeframe in the book is the Common Era, the past 2,000 years, when humans have dominated life on Earth. You address questions we are confronting today: How will warming affect El Nino or the Asian summer monsoons? Will the North Atlantic Ocean's conveyor-belt circulation change? Are our climate models underestimating the pace and extent of changes underway? Given all that, what worries you the most? What surprises you?**

A: What worries me the most is beyond the hockey stick. [The "hockey stick" was a graph published by Mann and others in 1999. It showed that the global average temperature was the same or slightly decreasing for more than 900 years and then turned sharply upward from the mid-1900s through 1999. It looked like a hockey stick laying on its side, with the blade at the far right pointing up in the air.] The obvious difference from past events is that we've warmed the climate so much faster during this timeframe. It turns out that El Nino, sea-level rise, and Arctic sea ice levels can all follow the hockey stick pattern. There's a theme: changes to some of these things are happening sooner than we expected.

One of these is the Atlantic meridional overturning circulation, or AMOC—the ocean conveyor belt. That's one of the surprises: the dramatic slowdown that we already see. There has been a dramatic slowdown in this circulation in the past century, even though the models say any slowdown should only occur during the upcoming next century. The blade of that hockey stick is coming about a century too early. One of the reasons is probably that we're losing Greenland ice faster, so we've got more fresh water already running off into the North Atlantic earlier than we expected.

Q: **What gives you the most hope?**
A: We don't know precisely how close we are to triggering some devastating tipping point that could threaten human civilization. The collective evidence from the past tells us that we've still got a safety margin. Science tells us that if we act quickly, if we act dramatically, we can avoid warming that will bring far worse consequences. That's the fragility of this moment: we have a little bit of a safety margin, but it's not a large safety margin. The phrase I use often these days, a phrase that characterizes the message of this book, is the pairing of urgency and agency. Yes, it's bad, and we face far worse consequences if we don't act. We can see devastating climate consequences already. That's the

urgency. But the paleoclimate record tells us we haven't triggered runaway warming yet. We can avoid that point of no return if we act quickly and dramatically. That's the agency. We've got 4 billion years of Earth history. Let's try to learn from it.

About the Author

Mark Fischetti has been a senior editor at Scientific American *for 17 years and has covered sustainability issues, including climate, weather, environment, energy, food, water, biodiversity, population, and more. He assigns and edits feature articles, commentaries and news by journalists and scientists and also writes in those formats. He edits History, the magazine's department looking at science advances throughout time. He was founding managing editor of two spinoff magazines:* Scientific American Mind *and* Scientific American Earth 3.0. *His 2001 freelance article for the magazine, "Drowning New Orleans," predicted the widespread disaster that a storm like Hurricane Katrina would impose on the city. His video* What Happens to Your Body after You Die? *has more than 12 million views on YouTube. Fischetti has written freelance articles for the* New York Times, Sports Illustrated, Smithsonian, Technology Review, Fast Company, *and many others. He co-authored the book* Weaving the Web *with Tim Berners-Lee, inventor of the World Wide Web, which tells the real story of how the Web was created. He also co-authored* The New Killer Diseases *with microbiologist Elinor Levy. Fischetti is a former managing editor of IEEE* Spectrum Magazine *and of* Family Business Magazine. *He has a physics degree and has twice served as the Attaway Fellow in Civic Culture at Centenary College of Louisiana, which awarded him an honorary doctorate. In 2021 he received the American Geophysical Union's Robert C. Cowen Award for Sustained Achievement in Science Journalism, which celebrates a career of outstanding reporting on the Earth and space sciences. He has appeared on NBC's* Meet the Press, *CNN, the History Channel, NPR News and many news radio stations. Follow Fischetti on X (formerly Twitter) @markfischetti*

Section 6: Nuclear War

South Asian Threat? Local Nuclear War = Global Suffering

By Alan Robock and Owen Brian Toon

Twenty-five years ago, international teams of scientists showed that a nuclear war between the U.S. and the Soviet Union could produce a "nuclear winter." The smoke from vast fires started by bombs dropped on cities and industrial areas would envelop the planet and absorb so much sunlight that the earth's surface would get cold, dark, and dry, killing plants worldwide and eliminating our food supply. Surface temperatures would reach winter values in the summer. International discussion about this prediction, fueled largely by astronomer Carl Sagan, forced the leaders of the two superpowers to confront the possibility that their arms race endangered not just themselves but the entire human race. Countries large and small demanded disarmament.

Nuclear winter became an important factor in ending the nuclear arms race. Looking back later, in 2000, former Soviet Union leader Mikhail S. Gorbachev observed, "Models made by Russian and American scientists showed that a nuclear war would result in a nuclear winter that would be extremely destructive to all life on Earth; the knowledge of that was a great stimulus to us, to people of honor and morality, to act."

Why discuss this topic now that the cold war has ended? Because as other nations continue to acquire nuclear weapons, smaller, regional nuclear wars could create a similar global catastrophe. New analyses reveal that a conflict between India and Pakistan, for example, in which 100 nuclear bombs were dropped on cities and industrial areas—only 0.4 percent of the world's more than 25,000 warheads—would produce enough smoke to cripple global agriculture. A regional war could cause widespread loss of life even in countries far away from the conflict.

Regional War Threatens the World

By deploying modern computers and modern climate models, the two of us and our colleagues have shown that not only were the ideas of the 1980s correct but the effects would last for at least 10 years, much longer than previously thought. And by doing calculations that assess decades of time, only now possible with fast, current computers, and by including in our calculations the oceans and the entire atmosphere—also only now possible—we have found that the smoke from even a regional war would be heated and lofted by the sun and remain suspended in the upper atmosphere for years, continuing to block sunlight and to cool the earth.

India and Pakistan, which together have more than 100 nuclear weapons, may be the most worrisome adversaries capable of a regional nuclear conflict today. But other countries besides the U.S. and Russia (which have thousands) are well endowed: China, France, and the U.K. have hundreds of nuclear warheads; Israel has more than 80, North Korea has about 10, and Iran may well be trying to make its own. In 2004 this situation prompted one of us (Toon) and later Rich Turco of the University of California, Los Angeles, both veterans of the 1980s investigations, to begin evaluating what the global environmental effects of a regional nuclear war would be and to take as our test case an engagement between India and Pakistan.

The latest estimates by David Albright of the Institute for Science and International Security and by Robert S. Norris of the Natural Resources Defense Council are that India has 50 to 60 assembled weapons (with enough plutonium for 100) and that Pakistan has 60 weapons. Both countries continue to increase their arsenals. Indian and Pakistani nuclear weapons tests indicate that the yield of the warheads would be similar to the 15-kiloton explosive yield (equivalent to 15,000 tons of TNT) of the bomb the U.S. used on Hiroshima.

Toon and Turco, along with Charles Bardeen, now at the National Center for Atmospheric Research, modeled what would happen if 50 Hiroshima-size bombs were dropped across the highest population-density targets in Pakistan and if 50 similar bombs were also dropped across India. Some people maintain that nuclear weapons would be used in only a measured way. But in the wake of chaos, fear and broken communications that would occur once a nuclear war began, we doubt leaders would limit attacks in any rational manner. This likelihood is particularly true for Pakistan, which is small and could be quickly overrun in a conventional conflict. Peter R. Lavoy of the Naval Postgraduate School, for example, has analyzed the ways in which a conflict between India and Pakistan might occur and argues that Pakistan could face a decision to use all its nuclear arsenal quickly before India swamps its military bases with traditional forces.

Obviously, we hope the number of nuclear targets in any future war will be zero, but policy makers and voters should know what is possible. Toon and Turco found that more than 20 million people in the two countries could die from the blasts, fires, and radioactivity—a horrible slaughter. But the investigators were shocked to discover that a tremendous amount of smoke would be generated, given the megacities in the two countries, assuming each fire would burn the same area that actually did burn in Hiroshima and assuming an amount of burnable material per person based on various studies. They calculated that the 50 bombs exploded in Pakistan would produce three teragrams of smoke, and the 50 bombs hitting India would generate four (one teragram equals a million metric tons).

Satellite observations of actual forest fires have shown that smoke can be lofted up through the troposphere (the bottom layer of the atmosphere) and sometimes then into the lower stratosphere (the layer just above, extending to about 30 miles). Toon and Turco also did some "back of the envelope" calculations of the possible climate impact of the smoke should it enter the stratosphere. The large magnitude of such effects made them realize they needed help from a climate modeler.

It turned out that one of us (Robock) was already working with Luke Oman, now at the NASA Goddard Space Flight Center, who was finishing his Ph.D. at Rutgers University on the climatic effects of volcanic eruptions, and with Georgiy L. Stenchikov, also at Rutgers and an author of the first Russian work on nuclear winter. They developed a climate model that could be used fairly easily for the nuclear blast calculations.

Robock and his colleagues, being conservative, put five teragrams of smoke into their modeled upper troposphere over India and Pakistan on an imaginary May 15. The model calculated how winds would blow the smoke around the world and how the smoke particles would settle out from the atmosphere. The smoke covered all the continents within two weeks. The black, sooty smoke absorbed sunlight, warmed, and rose into the stratosphere. Rain never falls there, so the air is never cleansed by precipitation; particles very slowly settle out by falling, with air resisting them. Soot particles are small, with an average diameter of only 0.1 micron (μm), and so drift down very slowly. They also rise during the daytime as they are heated by the sun, repeatedly delaying their elimination. The calculations showed that the smoke would reach far higher into the upper stratosphere than the sulfate particles that are produced by episodic volcanic eruptions. Sulfate particles are transparent and absorb much less sunlight than soot and are also bigger, typically 0.5 μm. The volcanic particles remain airborne for about two years, but smoke from nuclear fires would last a decade.

Killing Frosts in Summer

The climatic response to the smoke was surprising. Sunlight was immediately reduced, cooling the planet to temperatures lower than any experienced for the past 1,000 years. The global average cooling, of about 1.25 degrees Celsius (2.3 degrees Fahrenheit), lasted for several years, and even after 10 years the temperature was still 0.5 degree C colder than normal. The models also showed a 10 percent reduction in precipitation worldwide. Precipitation, river flow, and soil moisture all decreased because blocking sunlight reduces evaporation and weakens the hydrologic cycle. Drought was largely concentrated in the lower latitudes, however, because global cooling would retard the Hadley air circulation pattern in the tropics, which produces a large fraction of global precipitation. In critical areas such as the Asian monsoon regions, rainfall dropped by as much as 40 percent.

The cooling might not seem like much, but even a small dip can cause severe consequences. Cooling and diminished sunlight would, for example, shorten growing seasons in the midlatitudes. More insight into the effects of cooling came from analyses of the aftermaths of massive volcanic eruptions. Every once in a while such eruptions produce temporary cooling for a year or two. The largest of the past 500 years, the 1815 Tambora eruption in Indonesia, blotted the sun and produced global cooling of about 0.5 degree C for a year; 1816 became known as "The Year without a Summer" or "Eighteen Hundred and Froze to Death." In New England, although the average summer temperature was lowered only a few degrees, crop-killing frosts occurred in every month. After the first frost, farmers replanted crops, only to see them killed by the next frost. The price of grain skyrocketed, the price of livestock plummeted as farmers sold the animals they could not feed, and a mass migration began from New England to the Midwest, as people followed reports of fertile land there. In Europe the weather was so cold and gloomy that the stock market collapsed, widespread famines occurred, and 18-year-old Mary Shelley was inspired to write *Frankenstein*.

Certain strains of crops, such as winter wheat, can withstand lower temperatures, but a lack of sunlight inhibits their ability to grow. In our scenario, daylight would filter through the high smoky haze, but on the ground every day would seem to be fully overcast. Agronomists and farmers could not develop the necessary seeds or adjust agricultural practices for the radically different conditions unless they knew ahead of time what to expect.

In addition to the cooling, drying, and darkness, extensive ozone depletion would result as the smoke heated the stratosphere; reactions that create and destroy ozone are temperature-dependent. Michael J. Mills of the University of Colorado at Boulder ran a completely separate climate model from Robock's but found similar results for smoke lofting and stratospheric temperature changes. He concluded that although surface temperatures would cool by a small amount, the stratosphere would be heated by more than 50 degrees C, because the black smoke particles absorb sunlight. This heating, in turn, would modify winds in the stratosphere, which would carry ozone-destroying nitrogen oxides into its upper reaches. Together the high temperatures and nitrogen oxides would reduce ozone to the same dangerous levels we now experience below the ozone hole above Antarctica every spring. Ultraviolet radiation on the ground would increase significantly because of the diminished ozone.

Less sunlight and precipitation, cold spells, shorter growing seasons, and more ultraviolet radiation would all reduce or eliminate agricultural production. Notably, cooling and ozone loss would be most profound in middle and high latitudes in both hemispheres, whereas precipitation declines would be greatest in the tropics.

The specific damage inflicted by each of these environmental changes would depend on particular crops, soils, agricultural practices, and regional weather patterns, and no researchers have completed detailed analyses of such agricultural responses. Even in normal times, however, feeding the growing human population depends on transferring food across the globe to make up for regional farming deficiencies caused by drought and seasonal weather changes. The total amount of grain stored on the planet today would feed the earth's population for only about two months. Most cities and countries have stockpiled food supplies for just a very short period, and food shortages (as well as rising prices) have increased in recent years. A nuclear war could trigger declines in yield nearly everywhere at once, and a worldwide panic could bring the global agricultural trading system to a halt, with severe shortages in many places. Around 1 billion people worldwide who now live on marginal food supplies would be directly threatened with starvation by a nuclear war between India and Pakistan or between other regional nuclear powers.

Independent Evidence Needed

Typically scientists test models and theories by doing experiments, but we obviously cannot experiment in this case. Thus, we look for analogues that can verify our models.

- **Burned cities.** Unfortunately, firestorms created by intense releases of energy have pumped vast quantities of smoke into the upper atmosphere. San Francisco burned as a result of the 1906 earthquake, and whole cities were incinerated during World War II, including Dresden, Hamburg, Tokyo, Hiroshima, and Nagasaki. These events confirm that smoke from intense urban fires rises into the upper atmosphere.
- **The seasonal cycle.** In actual winter the climate is cooler because the days are shorter and sunlight is less intense; the simple change of seasons helps us quantify the effects of less solar radiation. Our climate models re-create the seasonal cycle well, confirming that they properly reflect changes in sunlight.
- **Eruptions.** Explosive volcanic eruptions, such as those of Tambora in 1815, Krakatau in 1883 and Pinatubo in 1991 provide several lessons. The resulting sulfate aerosol clouds that formed in the stratosphere were transported around the world by winds. The surface temperature plummeted after each eruption in proportion to the thickness of the particulate cloud. After the Pinatubo eruption, the global average surface temperature dropped by about 0.25 degree C. Global precipitation, river flow, and soil moisture all decreased. Our models reproduce these effects.
- **Forest fires.** Smoke from large forest fires sometimes is injected into the troposphere and lower stratosphere and is transported great distances, producing cooling. Our models perform well against these effects, too.
- **Extinction of the dinosaurs.** An asteroid smashed into Mexico's Yucatán Peninsula 65 million years ago. The resulting dust cloud, mixed with smoke from fires, blocked the sun, killing the dinosaurs. Massive volcanism in India at the same

time may have exacerbated the effects. The events teach us that large amounts of aerosols in the earth's atmosphere can change climate drastically enough to kill robust species.

We have used such analogues to test and improve our models in the past. But we hope more people will do further work. Independent models that either verify or contradict ours would be very instructive. Agricultural impact studies, which we have not conducted, would be particularly welcomed.

Abolition: The Only Policy

People have several incorrect impressions about nuclear winter. One is that the climatic effects were disproved; this is just not true. Another is that the world would experience "nuclear autumn" instead of winter. But our new calculations show that the climate effects even of a regional conflict would be widespread and severe. The models and computers used in the 1980s were not able to simulate the lofting and persistence of the smoke or the long time it would take oceans to warm back up as the smoke eventually dissipated; current models of a full-scale nuclear exchange predict a nuclear winter, not a nuclear fall.

Another misimpression is that the problem, even if it existed, has been solved by the end of the nuclear arms race. In fact, a nuclear winter could readily be produced by the American and Russian nuclear arsenals that are slated to remain in 2012. Furthermore, the increasing number of nuclear states raises the chances of a war starting deliberately or by accident. For example, North Korea has threatened war should the world stop its ships and inspect them for transporting nuclear materials. Fortunately, North Korea does not now have a usable nuclear arsenal, but it may have one capable of global reach in the near future. Some extremist leaders in India advocated attacking Pakistan with nuclear weapons following recent terrorist attacks on India. Because India could rapidly overrun Pakistan with conventional forces, it would be conceivable for Pakistan to attack India with nuclear weapons if it thought that India was about to go on the offensive. Iran has threatened to destroy Israel, already a nuclear power, which in turn has vowed never to allow Iran to become a nuclear state. Each of these examples represent countries that imagine their existence to be threatened completely and with little warning. These points of conflict have the potential to erupt suddenly.

The first nuclear war so shocked the world that in spite of the massive buildup of these weapons since then, they have never been used again. But the only way to eliminate the possibility of climatic catastrophe is to eliminate the weapons. Rapid reduction of the American and Russian arsenals would set an example for the rest of the world that nuclear weapons cannot be used and are not needed.

Under the Strategic Offensive Reductions Treaty, the U.S. and Russia both committed to reduce deployed strategic nuclear warheads down to between 1,700 to 2,200 apiece by the end of 2012. In July 2009 President Barack Obama and Russian president Dmitry Medvedev agreed to drop that range further, to 1,500 to 1,675 by 2016. Although smaller strategic arsenals are to be commended, our new results show that even the lower counts are far more than enough to destroy agriculture worldwide, as is a regional nuclear war. If this mother lode of weapons were used against urban targets, hundreds of millions of people would be killed and a whopping 180 Tg of smoke would be sent into the global stratosphere. Average temperatures would remain below freezing even in the summer for several years in major agricultural regions. Even the warheads on one missile-carrying submarine could produce enough smoke to create a global environmental disaster.

The combination of nuclear proliferation, political instability, and urban demographics may constitute one of the greatest dangers to the stability of society since the dawn of humans. Only abolition of nuclear weapons will prevent a potential nightmare. Immediate reduction of U.S. and Russian arsenals to the same levels as other nuclear powers (a few hundred) would maintain their deterrence, reduce the possibility of nuclear winter and encourage the rest of the world to continue to work toward the goal of elimination.

President Obama understands this logic. In his first press conference as president, on February 9, 2009, he said, "It is important for the United States, in concert with Russia ... to restart the conversations about how we can start reducing our nuclear arsenals in an effective way so that we then have the standing to go to other countries and start stitching back together the nonproliferation treaties." Then, on September 24, the president led the United Nations Security Council to approve a draft resolution that would step up efforts to rid the world of nuclear weapons. Our modeling results only strengthen the reasons to support further progress on such policy.

What Radioactive Fallout Tells Us about Our Nuclear Future

By Duy Linh Tu, Nina Berman, Sebastian Tuinder, Dominic Smith, Joseph Polidoro, and Jeffery DelViscio

Narrator: Twice a year thousands line up—many before dawn—in the middle of the New Mexico desert, just off of U.S. Highway 380.

They are *nuclear* tourists.

On July 16, 1945, the U.S. military detonated the first atomic bomb over this stretch of desert in New Mexico—a 24.8-kiloton blast code-named Trinity.

It was the culmination of the Manhattan Project, an all-out World War II effort by the U.S. military to build an atomic bomb before Germany did.

Although it was top secret, the blast could be felt 160 miles away. New scientific research shows that the fallout contaminated local residents, and spread radioactive particles across the U.S. and into Canada.

Soon after the test, the U.S. dropped two atomic bombs on the Japanese cities of Hiroshima and Nagasaki, killing more than 200,000 people. The war ended just days later.

Today that dark history seems lost on many of the visitors here.

But there are some here who are still dealing with the fallout of the Trinity test today.

These protesters are "downwinders," those who were *downwind* of the Trinity fallout. They say that radiation from the blast has caused cancer for generations of their families.

Mary White grew up near the Trinity test site.

Mary White: My mother died of metastasized cancer. My sister died of the same. Dad died of leukemia. I have a sister who is a breast cancer survivor. One sister who is a uterine cancer survivor.

It's the kind of thing that no one should ever have to experience, but we're experiencing it much too often here.

Narrator: And today, nearly 80 years after the Trinity test, the downwinders have a new fear. For the first time, after decades of arms reduction, the U.S. has started making nuclear weapons again.

The U.S. has embarked on the largest and most expensive nuclear build-out ever.

It's a project that will cost taxpayers trillions of dollars over decades. And most Americans, even many of those gathered here at the Trinity site, probably don't even know it's happening.

Sharon Weiner: Ask the average American what role nuclear weapons play, they're either going to tell you, "What do you mean 'we still have nuclear weapons'?"

Or if they think about it, they'll probably assert that they provide security, because there's this notion—it's almost like a national story we tell ourselves—that nuclear weapons are necessary for our security.

Narrator: The U.S. military says that the "modernization," as they call it, is necessary to replace an aging nuclear arsenal.

But critics argue that building these bombs comes with real risks, and even if the weapons are never used, making new warheads is dangerous and could lead to a repeat of previous environmental disasters.

Ty Neuman: The modernization effort that the United States is undergoing now is the largest modernization we've ever done in history.

Narrator: Brigadier General Ty Neuman is deputy director for plans and programs at the Air Force Global Strike Command.

He helped lead and shape the 2022 Nuclear Posture Review, a federally mandated report that establishes the country's nuclear policy, strategy, and capabilities.

Neuman says replacing the current nuclear arsenal with more sophisticated and powerful weapons is the military's top national security priority.

Neuman: We're now facing two nuclear peer adversaries that have or are building a significant nuclear enterprise of their own. In the case of the People's Republic of China, they're building a triad similar to ours.

Narrator: "Triad" refers to the three legs of the military's core nuclear strategy.

More than 1,700 warheads are currently deployed on 14 submarines, on 60 Air Force bombers, and in 400 intercontinental ballistic missiles, or ICBMs.

Each ICBM has a warhead with at least 20 times the destructive power of the atomic bomb dropped on Hiroshima.

These ICBMs, known as Minuteman IIIs, sit inside 450 underground silos spread across North Dakota, Montana, Wyoming, Colorado, and Nebraska.

And in the coming decade, each of the 450 silos will be replaced. The old missiles will be taken out, and new Sentinel ICBMs will be put back in.

Neuman: We think of the ICBM leg as the most responsive, being that the ICBMs are on alert 24/7, 365 days a year.

Narrator: But what the land leg does, more than any other part of the triad, is create targets in the U.S. where people live.

Weiner: U.S. ICBMs sit in silos in the ground. And we know that if the Russians and possibly the Chinese target those ICBMs, they'll destroy them. And so if you know this, and you know that Russian ICBMs can arrive in this country in 30 minutes or less, well, that means you have an incentive to launch them on warning.

Air Force Announcer: Item 132. Launch closure door open. 5...4...3...2...1...launch.

Weiner: And once the ICBMs are launched, they can't be recalled. They can't be destroyed in flight. They're going to their targets.

Narrator: Sharon Weiner is an associate professor, and a national security expert with a focus on nuclear weapons policy, at the School of International Service at American University.

Weiner: There are a whole variety of ways that system can mistake something for an incoming strike. And we know there have been hundreds of false alarms, hundreds of problems.

Nuclear weapons are outdated. What's more horrible than a nuclear weapon and the threat that you could kill not just yourself and your adversary, but everybody else who's not even involved in the conflict?

Neuman: It's the ultimate foundation. It's the, it's the, it's the safety mechanism. It's the insurance policy that we have that protects our Americans. And I applaud our policymakers and our administration for fully supporting this and getting behind it, as well as the continued funding from Congress.

Narrator: The original placement of the missile fields was decided during the Cold War. They needed to be close enough to reach Russia but, theoretically, far enough from major population centers.

But new research shows that if a modern-day adversary were to target them, the damage and fallout would affect millions more people than previously thought.

Sébastien Philippe: When you're attacking your missile silos with a nuclear weapon, you're essentially blowing up the ground creating those gigantic mushroom clouds, which carry the radioactivity of the nuclear explosion itself.

And these mushroom clouds get dispersed by, by the local winds. A lot of that radioactivity gets pushed by winds that have much higher speed, essentially, than what you experience on the ground, and so a larger amount of radioactivity gets dispersed over hundreds of miles downwind.

Narrator: Sébastien Philippe is a research scholar at Princeton University's Program on Science and Global Security focusing on nuclear weapons and emerging technologies.

Philippe's model uses atmospheric transport software to track millions of radioactive particles as they are dispersed by the winds.

Philippe: The scale of the potential impact was way bigger than any other representation that I had seen before.

Narrator: Earlier maps made by researchers and FEMA, the Federal Emergency Management Agency, used averaged wind data and averaged nuclear impacts, not worst-case scenarios.

But Philippe's work reveals the real cost of possible nuclear war.

Philippe: The radioactivity and the fallout from those weapons will cross the entire country—people living there would be at risk, one way or another, of receiving lethal doses of radiation.

Narrator: Nuclear modernization also means that the U.S. military is making warheads again, thousands of them, each with new radioactive triggers.

These triggers are called pits—hollow spheres of plutonium about the size of a bowling ball that make nuclear explosions possible.

Michael Ketterer: It is an assemblage of subcritical masses of plutonium, which is intended to be smashed together by chemical explosives to produce a supercritical mass, which then explodes in an uncontrolled fission reaction, producing a lot of energy, which then serves as the trigger for a thermonuclear explosion.

Narrator: Michael Ketterer specializes in environmental chemistry.

He is professor emeritus at Northern Arizona University.

These days, he spends most of his time in the field measuring and monitoring soil for plutonium contamination.

Ketterer: As a result of nuclear weapons tests, plutonium is found pretty much everywhere on Earth's surface. So the default condition that we should expect in surface soils is perhaps about one picogram per gram. That kind of concentration of plutonium can be expected here and there and everywhere.

Ketterer (tape): It's just in this top part of the mineral soil that the highest activity of the plutonium is usually found.

Narrator: Ketterer is looking at the fallout from our nuclear past that has lain hidden and undocumented.

Yet it is still dangerous decades after it was blown into the atmosphere—or leaked into the groundwater.

Ketterer: If you were to look at, say, a map of the whole continental U.S. or a map of the whole world, there are a few hotspots, so to speak, where there's quite a bit more plutonium can be found. Rocky Flats is one of those hotspots. It's one of the most prominent hotspots in the continental United States

Narrator: Rocky Flats, Colorado, 16 miles northwest of Denver, was home to a 6,500-acre nuclear weapons manufacturing complex. It operated from 1952 until its formal closure in 1992.

Today little remains of the plant that produced 70,000 plutonium pits during its operation.

Most of the land around it has been turned into Rocky Flats nature reserve, yet million-dollar houses have sprung up over the past several years around the edges of the reserve.

The only indication of its nuclear past is a local artist's sculpture of a horse in a hazmat suit.

It's called "Cold War Horse," and it's dedicated to those who became ill and died working at Rocky Flats.

But for Ketterer and others who are skeptical of the U.S.'s nuclear modernization effort, what happened in Rocky Flats is a sharp warning of what could happen again as the country ramps up its plutonium pit production.

The production facility at Rocky Flats manufactured the plutonium pits along with depleted uranium components for weapons. This generated tons of radioactive waste at the plant.

Jon Lipsky: From 1951 to 1975, there was actually no plan for the waste. The U.S. government did not have a policy about nuclear waste disposal.

Narrator: Jon Lipsky is a former FBI agent. He led an unprecedented raid on the Rocky Flats plant in 1989 for violating environmental protection rules.

Lipsky: The nuclear waste disposition was both open air incineration, like little barbecues on the, on the site. They would just burn the waste and hope for it to go away. And then, also, barrels were filled with aqueous waste. And that waste had nowhere to go except in the backyard.

Ketterer: The plutonium-laden cutting, cutting oils were placed in these steel drums. They were set out in the elements and essentially abandoned. Over time corrosion resulted in some of the drums rupturing, and this contaminated oil leaked out onto the soil, which then, through the action of wind and water, got spread in the environment.

Narrator: In 1992 the plant was closed. A year later the Department of Energy revealed that the Rocky Flats site contained at least 14 tons of plutonium, seven tons of enriched uranium, 281 tons of depleted uranium and 65 tons of beryllium.

After a $7-billion dollar,10-year cleanup effort, the Environmental Protection Agency declared the area safe in 2006. Early estimates said it would take nearly $40 billion dollars and 65 years.

Lipsky: What is now the refuge, the National Wildlife Refuge, was never touched. No action was taken. That means nothing was done. And the 20,000 acres—nothing was done. There's no action. They weren't cleaned up.

Narrator: But ground and groundwater contamination were not the only threats to the area. Two major fires at the plant, in 1957 and 1969, had already sent plutonium particles into the air. And winds spread them for miles.

Ketterer continues to find high plutonium contamination readings throughout the Rocky Flats area.

Ketterer: There's two things that you always see: there's elevated activities or concentrations of plutonium—there's more than you expect in Earth's nuclear weapons test fallout background, and the plutonium is specifically attributable to Rocky Flats.

Narrator: With Rocky Flats closed, the U.S. military has returned to New Mexico, to the Los Alamos National Laboratory, or LANL, to restart its pit production program.

Billions have been earmarked for the production of new plutonium pits. To begin, the military had to rebuild and restart the LANL site, as well as the Savannah River plant in South Carolina.

The goal is to make 80 new pits per year by 2030: 30 at LANL and 50 at Savannah River.

At this pace, by 2080, all 4,000 nuclear weapons in the U.S. arsenal will have new nuclear pits installed.

But delays at the Savannah River site mean that LANL is the only facility in operation, and production is already behind schedule.

No plutonium pits have been made in the U.S. since 2013, and LANL's Plutonium Facility Four, or PF-4, was previously set up as a research lab, not a manufacturing plant.

Robert Webster is deputy director of weapons at LANL. He's in charge of all pit production and, in many ways, the core of the nuclear modernization effort.

Robert Webster: Yeah, there's a ton of pressure to try to get to that 30 pit per year, and, and really, there's a ton of pressure nationally to get to 80 pits per year as quickly as we can.

It's a massive undertaking, both to transform PF-4 into having this branch, which is a production branch, in it.

When you're dealing with very hazardous material like this, you're having to add criticality safety engineers and safety basis design. You have to up the number of health [physicians] in the laboratories that monitor whether people have been exposed to anything.

Narrator: Webster says the rationale for rapid pit production is that the military fears the plutonium in old pits is aging, making weapons potentially unstable or ineffective. That's why they have to move fast.

But some argue that new pit production is unnecessary.

Most of the active pits are only about 40 years old.

In 2006 a study by JASON, a group of independent scientific advisers to the government, said that pits could last for 100 years or more.

Jay Coghlan: So we don't truly know how long pits might last. I don't think the government wants an updated pit lifetime study because its conclusion would run counter to this very aggressive $60 billion program to expand plutonium pit production.

Narrator: Jay Coghlan is director of Nuclear Watch New Mexico, a nonprofit watchdog group that advocates for consistent U.S. leadership toward a world free of nuclear weapons.

Jay Coghlan (tape): Why is nuclear disarmament necessary? We survived the Cuban missile crisis only by luck. Luck is not a sustainable strategy, especially when we're talking about civilization-ending weapons.

Narrator: In 2019, however, JASON released another report that reversed its previous statement. The group said that there was uncertainty to plutonium pit aging and recommended further study.

At LANL, like in Rocky Flats, the plutonium is handled by humans in glove boxes. Webster says that the safety mistakes made at Rocky Flats loom over his operation.

Webster: We are very well aware of that legacy. That would lead to, ultimately, in my opinion, to a choice of disarmament that we can't afford to make.

Narrator: But on May 18, 2023, the National Nuclear Security Administration cited Triad National Security, a private contractor at LANL, for significant lack of attention and carelessness in protecting workers and the public.

The report detailed four nuclear safety events, including one glove box breach, and flooding. The fear with flooding is that water can enhance fission, causing plutonium to go critical.

According to SearchLight New Mexico, an independent investigative news organization, LANL has recorded 95 "process deviations" over the last five years, including safety incidents, emergency events, and protocol violations.

Webster says that the high numbers of incidents is a result of increased transparency at the lab.

Webster: This is why we encourage reporting. This is why our folks don't get in trouble when they report these low-level things. This is why we take sometimes the hits out in, out in the public world with the number of incidents that are going on.

If I ever shut down that reporting, I run the risk of becoming Rocky Flats. And we will not do that while I'm here.

Narrator: Webster also has to deal with the nuclear waste LANL will produce. The current plan is to ship waste to the Waste Isolation Pilot Plant, or WIPP, near Carlsbad, New Mexico.

There it will be stored 2,150 feet under the ground...permanently.

But in 2014 a faulty waste shipment from LANL caused a fire at WIPP, which shut the facility for three years and cost $2 billion dollars to clean up.

Ketterer: The plutonium waste from pit production—we can expect those to be dangerous for well, at least 10 half-lifes of plutonium 239. So that's putting it at about a quarter of a million years. It's unimaginable that humans can contain things on that kind of timescale.

Narrator: On this night, the anniversary of the original Trinity test, Mary White and other downwinders are holding what has become an annual event.

It is a vigil in remembrance of those downwinders who have died of cancer.

And it also recognizes the long shadow nuclear weapons have cast over their community.

Woman at Ceremony: On July 16, 1945, they detonated the bomb at the Trinity site. We started this 13 years ago to memorialize the people that we've lost in our communities as a result of being overexposed to radiation.

White (tape): Bobby Gonzales. Elizabeth Gonzales. Eloy Gonzales. Gilbert Gonzales. Ruth Tyler. Bennie Flores.

About the Authors

Duy Linh Tu is a journalist and documentary filmmaker focusing on education, science and social justice. His work has appeared in print and online, on television and in theaters. He is also author of Feature and Narrative Storytelling for Multimedia Journalists *(Focal Press). And he teaches reporting and video storytelling courses at the Columbia University Graduate School of Journalism. Follow him on X (formerly Twitter) @duylinhtu.*

Nina Berman is a documentary photographer, filmmaker, journalist and educator. Her work explores American politics, militarism, environmental issues and post violence trauma. She is a tenured Professor of Journalism at Columbia University Graduate School of Journalism where she directs the photojournalism/documentary photography program.

Sebastian Tuinder is a multimedia journalist with an eye for cinematic storytelling. He prides himself on creating films that are both informative and beautiful.

Dominic Smith is an Emmy winning multimedia producer, visual effects artist and journalist based in New Hampshire. He operates Smith Robinson Multimedia with offices in New England and California.

Jeff DelViscio is currently Chief Multimedia Editor/Executive Producer at Scientific American. He is former director of multimedia at STAT, where he oversaw all visual, audio and interactive journalism. Before that, he spent over eight years at the New York Times, where he worked on five different desks across the paper. He holds dual master's degrees from Columbia in journalism and in earth and environmental sciences. He has worked aboard oceanographic research vessels and tracked money and politics in science from Washington, D.C. He was a Knight Science Journalism Fellow at MIT in 2018. His work has won numerous awards, including two News and Documentary Emmy Awards.

Section 7: Cosmic Endings

Will Pluto Be the Last Habitable World?

By Caleb A. Scharf

Astronomers often talk about our sun's future and how it will likely bring about the end of Earth. Specifically: like all hydrogen-fusing stars, the sun gets gradually brighter with time as it converts more and more hydrogen in its core into helium (changing its own composition and therefore central temperature). But it will also eventually get to a point where the central hydrogen runs out, the core contracts, and the rest of the star responds. In what's termed the Red-Giant-Branch (RGB) stage, the outer envelope of the sun will begin to inflate—growing over 100 times in radius over less than 100 million years if it doesn't lose too much material.

At this point it's bye-bye to Mercury and Venus (even if their orbits expand due to stellar mass loss, as I talk about below). But eventually the sun will shrink again. This happens when its core of helium starts fusing, once more altering the balance and flow of energy in the star. Later, just as the core hydrogen ran out, the helium in the core will also run out—resulting in a new inflation of the outer envelope. This time the sun gets even bigger. As an Asymptotic-Giant-Branch (AGB) object its radius might crank up to nearly a thousand times the present solar dimensions. Now it's a distinct possibility that Earth and Mars get engulfed.

Except some other stuff is also happening throughout these phases. Energy is still being generated by fusion in shell regions around the core, and the sun is in fact going to lose quite a lot of its mass—literally blowing material away in a strengthened solar wind. This may mute the physical diameter it reaches as an RGB and then AGB star, but not by a great deal. It could be enough to save Earth and Mars though. Because as the sun loses mass the orbits of the planets will actually expand in order to conserve angular momentum.

Another critical factor for our planetary system is that the larger the surface area of a star the larger its luminosity—the total power it can push out as electromagnetic radiation. By the time the sun gets into its RGB and AGB phases, its luminosity can grow to a thousand or even several thousand times its present value.

We can work out what this might do to the nominal temperature of other bodies in the system. The bottom line is that their temperature should increase roughly like the fourth-root of solar luminosity. That means that they'll get hotter by anywhere from a factor of 2 to perhaps a factor of 7 or 8 depending on the stellar output. The first round of this heating will come during the RGB stellar phase. It'll then get cold again until the AGB phase kicks in, after which it'll reach its second, and utterly final peak.

For fun we can take a look at the implications for icy, chemically rich objects like Europa, Titan, and good old Pluto. The question to ask is—who's last? Which is the final potentially habitable body within the most familiar orbital terrain of our solar system?

Today the icy moon Europa has an equatorial surface temperature of around 110 Kelvin (-163 Celsius). That means that it could get as hot as over 770 Kelvin (497 Celsius) by the time the sun has reached the end of its AGB phase, and perhaps even during the earlier RGB phase. Naturally there will be intermediate periods where things might be more temperate, but as the stellar clock ticks Europa will get seriously hot.

Further away is Titan, a place with lots of frozen water and a hydrocarbon-rich surface environment—if there was ever a place that might get really interesting with a heat-spell it would be Titan. If Titan's surface is about 94 Kelvin (-179 Celsius) today it might certainly warm up to a temperate state. But like Europa, as the sun gets to its maximum luminosity we'd expect Titan to hit as high as about 680 Kelvin (407 Celsius). That's not so comfy.

Pluto is a slightly different story. In the present-day solar system Pluto is coated in frozen everything: Solid water, solid carbon monoxide, solid nitrogen, solid methane, all at a chilly 43 Kelvin (-230 Celsius). But by the time the sun reaches peak luminosity (during its RGB and then AGB stages) Pluto may warm up to an acceptably habitable 300 Kelvin (27 Celsius). On the way to that peak it might spend millions of years between the freezing and boiling point of water (assuming a thick atmosphere).

Of course, as a frozen object gets heated it will lose a lot of sublimated material to the vacuum of space. Water, carbon monoxide, and so on will just stream away. However, even a low gravitational surface acceleration like Pluto's (about 1/12th of Earth's) will cause some buildup of atmosphere. And atmosphere is good at encouraging more atmosphere; by making it harder for molecules to make it from the surface to space. In other words, Pluto could develop a thicker envelope, and conceivably much more clement conditions.

All of this new-found status would be fleeting though. Pluto would have at best a few hundred thousand, or possibly a million or two years to bask in the glory of being the last habitable world of the solar system. After that it too would return to the eternal cold of the cosmos.

This article was published in Scientific American's *former blog network and reflects the views of the author, not necessarily those of* Scientific American.

About the Author

Caleb A. Scharf is a researcher and writer. He is the senior scientist for astrobiology at NASA's Ames Research Center in Silicon Valley.

Can Lucky Planets Get a Second Chance at Life?

By Conor Feehly

For decades, astronomers have endeavored to forecast with confidence the fate of planetary systems, including our own, throughout the cosmos. And these experts' predictions have one central principle: to confidently guess what will eventually befall a planet, you have to know the size of its star.

Tiny stars don't really burn out but rather fade away as they shine dimly for hundreds of billions or even trillions of years, likely keeping their planetary companions in tow. Massive stars go out with a bang, expiring as a supernova that leaves behind a neutron star or black hole. Such events tend to be cataclysmic for planetary systems. And stars of middling mass, like our own, expand into a red giant, engulfing or scorching their planets and then dissipating to become a slow-cooling stellar ember called a white dwarf.

This dismal fate is expected to befall our sun in some 5 billion years, setting what has been considered the last-gasp expiration date for life on Earth and perhaps throughout the solar system.

But insights from fresh studies of dying stars and doomed worlds elsewhere in the Milky Way challenge this consensus. Increasingly, it seems that the eventual fates of planetary systems, ours included, are not wholly written in the stars.

Specifically, two new findings—the discovery of a giant planet closely orbiting around a red giant star and the identification and estimation of the number of so-called rogue planets adrift in our galaxy—have highlighted that there are many more nuanced scenarios to consider. Planets can survive the ruin of their star, and the vast majority of planetary systems shed numerous worlds throughout their history.

The Planet That Shouldn't Exist

When our sun eventually enters its red giant phase, its radius will likely extend well beyond Earth's present-day orbit. Even if our planet and the solar system's other inner rocky worlds escape engulfment, the sun's swelling will probably still spell their end because of the scorching temperatures they will experience. For the former scenario, astronomers have been seeing signs of this demise in the atmospheres of white dwarfs: researchers have found such stars littered with the remnants of dead planets they likely swallowed.

In fact, astronomers believed the fate of any planet orbiting a star within its red giant radius was likely sealed. That was until the discovery of the planet 8 Ursae Minoris b (8 UMi b), also known as Halla (after the South Korean mountain Hallasan and in honor of the South Korean astronomers who initially identified it in 2015).

"We used to think that planets just couldn't survive around stars that become red giants—but this system provides a loophole," explains Malena Rice, an assistant professor of astrophysics at Yale University, who co-authored new research on Halla postulating how it improbably survived.

Halla was discovered by the wobbling its orbital tugging induced on its red giant home star, 8 Ursae Minoris (8 UMi). Track the period of that wobble over time, and you can discern the length of a planet's year and its distance from its star. Such scrutiny showed that Halla orbits a mere 75 million kilometers from 8 UMi—that is, just half the distance between Earth and the sun. But standard modeling of 8 UMi's red giant phase suggested that the star's puffy, hot stellar atmosphere should have expanded about 30 million km farther out than that at its swollen peak. That is, Halla appeared to be a planet that shouldn't exist. It should've been consumed and obliterated. Instead it had somehow escaped.

"This planet was very lucky," Rice says. "In its past, we think that it may have orbited two stars rather than one, and this helped it to survive what could have been a fiery fate."

Binary stars can exchange material back and forth, and they can even merge to become a single star, allowing a rich diversity of novel possibilities for any orbiting worlds. Such major redistributions of mass can alter planetary orbits while also profoundly influencing how a star shines, adding or siphoning away gas to change the nature and timing of its subsequent stellar evolution. According to the careful modeling work of Rice and her colleagues, the most likely explanation for Halla's survival is that 8 UMi was once accompanied by a smaller close-in companion star, with which it eventually merged. Among other effects, the merger would've stifled 8 UMi's red giant expansion, sparing Halla.

Although this mechanism clarifies how some fortunate worlds might survive their star's antics, it offers scant hope for our own solar system because our sun lacks a stellar companion to tamp down its eventual evolutionary swelling.

"It will be tough for our rocky planets to make it through that process if the sun swells beyond their orbits," Rice says. "But perhaps finding more systems like these might teach us about interesting natural 'loopholes' that occur in at least some types of planetary systems."

Rogue Worlds by the Trillions

Bountiful discoveries of newfound worlds—and with them, perhaps, the revelation of more "loopholes"—could come relatively soon via NASA's Nancy Grace Roman Space Telescope, which is due to launch by May 2027. Much of Roman's potential comes from its planned exoplanet survey, which will rely on a relatively underused technique known as microlensing. In this method, Roman will stare at many stars simultaneously, looking for instances where, by chance, a planet-bearing star will be perfectly aligned to cross in front of another "background" star much farther away. In such cases, some of the foreground star's planets can act as gravitational lenses and magnify the background star's light in a way that allows astronomers to reconstruct a lensing world's mass and orbit. The technique is especially sensitive to planets orbiting far from their stars—a circumstellar region that remains scarcely probed by other planet-hunting methods.

And in fact, it's also capable of finding worlds that have left their stars behind entirely—something Roman could leverage to discover hundreds of rogue planets in interstellar space. Already preexisting microlensing surveys have found a handful of these free-floating worlds, and the statistics of this largely hidden population suggest most planetary systems have a surprisingly turbulent history.

The latest example comes from the MOA (Microlensing Observations in Astrophysics) survey, a project conducted at the University of Canterbury Mt. John Observatory on New Zealand's South Island by an international team, including scientists at NASA and Japan's Osaka University. Running for almost a decade, MOA has gathered enough data to weigh in on the galactic abundance of rogue planets down to and even below Earth mass.

"This number turns out to be somewhat larger than we would have guessed," says David Bennett, a senior research scientist at NASA's Goddard Space Flight Center and co-author of two new papers reporting on these findings that were posted on the preprint server arXiv.org. These papers are set to be published in a future issue of the *Astronomical Journal*.

So far MOA has only detected six microlensing events that are consistent with magnification by a low-mass rogue planet, says MOA collaborator Takahiro Sumi, a professor at Osaka University, who co-authored both preprint studies. "Taking into account the low detection efficiency and our detections, we estimated that there are many such low-mass objects in the galaxy," he adds.

"We found that there are about 20 free-floating planets per star in the galaxy, and the number is dominated by low-mass planets with a mass similar to or smaller than that of Earth," Bennett says. Those numbers, in turn, suggest an astounding 2 trillion rogue worlds in the Milky Way alone—six times more than the planets that are estimated to be bound to stars.

If this estimate is correct, it means most planetary systems are essentially dissolving across cosmic time, jettisoning many of their members via dynamical interactions between planets or their host stars that can slingshot unlucky worlds out into the interstellar abyss. It's possible that when we look out into the solar system and other multiplanetary systems, the remaining planets we see are rare vestiges of once-bustling neighborhoods.

Bennett explains that most rogue worlds likely get ejected during the early stages of planetary formation, after which planetary systems settle into more stable configurations. The probability of ejections should generally decrease throughout a sunlike star's life, he says. But when it swells into a red giant and begins shedding its outer layers of gas, the resulting shifts in planetary orbits can spark new rounds of world-ejecting instabilities.

Stars that are much heavier than the sun and end their life as a supernova, Bennett suggests, could also provide a rich source of rogue worlds and help to explain MOA's outsize estimates.

Scott Gaudi, an astronomer and microlensing expert at the Ohio State University, thinks MOA's surprising results are the best currently available but cautions that they remain very uncertain, so they "should be taken with a grain of salt." Roman, he says, should beef up the statistical certitude, thanks to the unprecedented sensitivity of its prospective microlensing survey.

The Question of Life

If MOA's estimates are accurate, however, the sheer number of rogue worlds raises an interesting question: Could any of them provide conditions favorable to life? Ravi Kopparapu, a planetary habitability expert at NASA's Goddard Space Flight Center, says life on a rogue planet would be problematic—but not impossible.

"Without a star, life on a cold rogue world would likely need to get its energy from internal sources," Kopparapu says. "That could be in the form of tidal/frictional heat like in some of Jupiter's moons where there are subsurface oceans, from residual energy when the planet formed or from the radioactive decay of heavy elements in the planet's core." Such worlds might resemble the large moons of our outer solar system and harbor potentially clement conditions beneath an icy crust.

For surface habitability, Kopparapu says a thick hydrogen atmosphere could possibly insulate a rogue planet and keep its surface temperature warm enough for living things to endure. Such atmospheres are easily blown away by stellar radiation, but because rogue planets do not orbit stars, they might be able to cling to an insulating atmosphere of hydrogen far longer than any sunbathed world could.

Amid so much uncertainty, life's prospects in such alien environments can seem either dizzying or dim. Might biospheres someday be found eking out existence around post-red giant stars or on worlds without a star at all? The thought is staggering, to say the least—and the fact that we could soon have real data to better answer such grand questions is all the more so.

About the Author

Conor Feehly is a New Zealand based writer who covers topics ranging from astronomy to consciousness studies and the philosophy of science. His work has appeared in New Scientist, Discover, Nautilus, Live Science *and many other publications.*

Planets Orbiting Dead Stars Foretell the Solar System's Far-Future Fate

By Phil Plait

In the distant future—about 6 billion or 7 billion years hence—the sun will start to die, swelling up into a bloated red giant. In a span of several hundred million years it will blow away its outer layers, lose about half its mass and leave behind its überhot, überdense, super small core: a white dwarf.

The inner planets will be toast when this happens. Mercury, Venus, and most likely even our precious Earth will be literally consumed by the sun and vaporized as their once benevolent host star literally overruns and engulfs them. But what of the outer planets, such as Jupiter and Saturn? They should survive the ordeal, being so far removed from the solar system's center. Until now, though, there was scant direct observational evidence that such outer worlds can endure the death throes of their sunlike stellar host.

Using the James Webb Space Telescope (JWST), a team of astronomers led by Susan Mullally at the Space Telescope Science Institute targeted four white dwarfs, hoping to get direct images of any large planets that might still orbit them. Two came up empty, but the other two show evidence of extant giant exoplanets still orbiting them. To be clear, these planets have not yet been confirmed, but if the research pans out, they will act as a glimpse into the future of our sun and its worlds—and that future is not exactly a comforting one. The group's research, which was posted to the preprint server arXiv.org last month, has been accepted for publication in the *Astrophysical Journal Letters*.

The four white dwarfs were chosen for JWST's scrutiny because there seemed to be good chances that they had possessed planets in their pre-red-giant phases—and that any planets still lingering around them should be straightforward to see. They're relatively near to the sun in the galaxy, making planets around them easier to spot; from too far away the planets and host stars would blend into a single blob. Also, these white dwarfs are young enough that any extant planets should still be glowing in the infrared from the leftover heat of their formation—that is, the younger they are, the warmer they are and the easier JWST can spot them.

Most importantly, though, previous observations revealed that all four white dwarfs have surfaces polluted with heavy elements. White dwarfs are small but massive. They're about the size of Earth but about half as massive as the sun. This gives them a ferocious surface gravity that is 100,000 times that of Earth. Any heavy elements such as calcium or iron should sink rapidly in their hot hydrogen and helium plasma soup—very rapidly, even within a matter of days. If any elements like that are seen, then, it's almost certainly because the white dwarf has very recently dined on a snack of asteroids composed of those elements. We know in our own solar system that gravitational interactions with the giant planets commonly fling asteroids and comets down toward the sun. If that happens in other stellar systems—and there's no reason to suppose that it doesn't—then seeing those heavy elements smeared across the surface of a white dwarf implies the existence of big, unseen worlds further out from the star.

JSWT is perfect for this search because in visible light, like what Hubble or most ground-based telescopes primarily detect, stars are millions or even billions of times brighter than any of their planets. In infrared the contrast is lower. On top of that, white dwarfs are so hot that they emit most of their light in ultraviolet, making them even fainter yet in infrared, where they may be only a factor of a hundred or so times brighter than a giant planet—easy pickings.

After the astronomers processed and analyzed the images, two of the white dwarf targets, WD 1202-232 and WD 2105-82, appeared to have faint companion objects close by. The estimated ages of these stars are 5.3 billion and 1.6 billion years, respectively. But that includes their extensive histories before entering their white-dwarf denouement. Both made that transition 900 million to 800 million years ago, so they are indeed young, astronomically speaking.

The two candidate companions each have an infrared brightness consistent with that of large gas-giant planets of approximately the same age as their host star. Their mass, inferred from their brightness across multiple wavelengths, is one to seven and one to two times the mass of Jupiter, respectively—firmly in the "planetary" mass range. This rules out the possibility that they are brown dwarfs.

Their orbital distances are very interesting. WD 1202-232's candidate companion is about 1.8 billion kilometers out from the star, and WD 2105-82's is even farther away, at circa 5.2 billion kilometers. Those far-flung positions are very unlikely to be where these putative worlds started out, however; as stars die and lose mass, their gravitational grip on their planets weakens, and the planets migrate farther out as a result. This means they probably originated closer in, around 800 million and 1.5 billion kilometers, respectively, from their stars. That's very similar to the current distances of Jupiter and Saturn from the sun!

If confirmed, these planets would show that the outer planets in our own solar system may very well survive the sun's demise, even if the inner planets most likely will not.

JWST's observations also lend support to the hypothesis that giant planets toss asteroids down to their white dwarf host. If no planets at all were found around any of the four target stars, this idea would be weakened; it would potentially imply that perhaps only smaller planets, invisible to JWST, feed their star in this way. (Such small planets, I should note, could still be lurking around the other two white dwarfs where no giant planets were seen.)

But let's not be too hasty; once again, these planets are not yet confirmed. From their color, the astronomers could rule out these objects being distant stars or objects in our own solar system. They could be very distant red background galaxies, but given how many are seen in the images, the chance of two of them being so apparently close to the white dwarfs is low. The odds are about one in 3,000, according to the astronomers' calculations. That finding is inconclusive but hopeful.

The best way to confirm them is to take more observations in the near future. The white dwarfs are moving through space and will be seen to change their position relative to background stars. If these objects are truly planets, they will move along with the stars; if they're background objects, they'll appear fixed. The uncertainty is certainly frustrating at this moment, but time will tell.

Given the seeming success of these observations, though, hopefully JWST will be monitoring more white dwarfs soon to see if other potential planetary survivors can be found and, with them, more insight into the fate of our own solar system.

Of course, we could just wait 6 billion or 7 billion years to see what'll happen. But I'd prefer to know sooner, while we still have an unvaporized planet to study it from.

About the Author

Phil Plait is a professional astronomer and science communicator in Virginia. He writes the Bad Astronomy Newsletter.

GLOSSARY

acute Especially severe, sharp, or significant.

amateur Lacking formal certification or training.

anaerobic Biological processes that do not require the presence of oxygen.

chronic disease A disease that persists for at least several months and is typically not curable.

collision course When an object's force and momentum are predicted to result in an impact with another object.

demise Death or destruction.

disarmament The process of mutually removing or destroying weapons of war.

emission Releasing something, typically energy or gases.

endemic To be widespread in an area, often used to describe diseases.

epidemiology The study of how a disease spreads.

fallout The aftereffects of a nuclear explosion, especially persistent radiation.

hypothetical A scenario that is imagined rather than actually existing.

inimical Counterproductive or harmful.

innate Determined by something's origin or makeup, rather than its external surroundings.

kiloton A measure of explosive power equivalent to one thousand tons of TNT, often used for classifying nuclear weapons.

mitigation Efforts to reduce the negative effect of something.

paleoclimatology The study of climate change on the scale of millions of years.

Pangaea The name of the single continent on Earth hundreds of millions of years ago, before breaking up into the continents we now know.

pathogen A microbe or other living being that causes disease.

plasma A state of matter characterized by high temperatures and freely floating electrons.

positive feedback loop When the effects of a process make that process still more severe.

proliferate To spread widely or flourish.

Ragnarok Scandinavian mythological concept of the end of the world.

rust A fungal disease that especially affects the leaves of plants.

somber Mournful, sad, or serious.

strata A layer of geological material, characterized by the epoch of its formation.

FURTHER INFORMATION

"National Preparedness," Federal Emergency Management Agency (FEMA), https://www.fema.gov/emergency-managers/national-preparedness.

"Preparing for Pandemics," World Health Organization (WHO), https://www.who.int/westernpacific/activities/preparing-for-pandemics.

"Special Report: Global Warming of 1.5 ºC," Intergovernmental Panel on Climate Change (IPCC), https://www.ipcc.ch/sr15/.

Horgan, John. "Can Science Survive the Death of the Universe?," *Scientific American*, June 16, 2021, https://www.scientificamerican.com/article/can-science-survive-the-death-of-the-universe/.

Metcalfe, Tom. "The Roman Empire's Worst Plagues Were Linked to Climate Change," *Scientific American*, January 26, 2024, https://www.scientificamerican.com/article/the-roman-empires-worst-plagues-were-linked-to-climate-change/.

Parshall, Allison. "Could the Zombie Fungus in TV's *The Last of Us* Really Infect People?," *Scientific American*, February 10, 2023, https://www.scientificamerican.com/article/could-the-zombie-fungus-in-tvs-the-last-of-us-really-infect-people/.

Parshley, Lois. "When Disaster Strikes, Is Climate Change to Blame?," *Scientific American*, June 1, 2023, https://www.scientificamerican.com/article/when-disaster-strikes-is-climate-change-to-blame/.

Weber, Ella. "What Would It Mean to 'Absorb' a Nuclear Attack?," *Scientific American*, November 22, 2023, https://www.scientificamerican.com/podcast/episode/what-would-it-mean-to-absorb-a-nuclear-attack/.

CITATIONS

1.1 How the Stress of Disaster Brings People Together by Emma Seppala (November 6, 2012); 1.2 Psychology Reveals the Comforts of the Apocalypse by Daisy Yuhas (December 18, 2012); 1.3 Fix Disaster Response Now by The Editors of Scientific American (September 1, 2023); 1.4 Will Humans Ever Go Extinct? by Stephanie Pappas (March 21, 2023); 2.1 What Ancient Mass Extinctions Tell Us about the Future by Peter Brannen (September 1, 2020); 2.2 Dinosaur Asteroid Hit Worst-Case Place by Julia Rosen (October 22, 2020); 2.3 Toxic Slime Contributed to Earth's Worst Mass Extinction—And It's Making a Comeback by Chris Mays, Vivi Vajda & Stephen McLoughlin (July 1, 2022); 3.1 Stopping Deforestation Can Prevent Pandemics by The Editors of Scientific American (June 1, 2020); 3.2 Deadly Fungi Are the Newest Emerging Microbe Threat All Over the World by Maryn McKenna (June 1, 2021); 3.3 How Mathematics Can Predict—And Help Prevent—The Next Pandemic by Rachel Crowell (April 6, 2023); 4.1 Are We Doing Enough to Protect Earth from Asteroids? by Sarah Scoles (June 1, 2021); 4.2 NASA's DART Spacecraft Successfully Smacks a Space Rock—Now What? by Jonathan O'Callaghan (September 26, 2022); 4.3 NASA Asteroid Threat Practice Drill Shows We're Not Ready by Matt Brady (November 4, 2022); 5.1 There's Still Time to Fix Climate—About 11 Years by Mark Fischetti (October 27, 2021); 5.2 Extreme Heat Is Deadlier Than Hurricanes, Floods and Tornadoes Combined by Terri Adams-Fuller (July 1, 2023); 5.3 Carbon in the Oceans Is Altering the Micro-Fabric of Life by David Ewing Duncan (September 8, 2023); 5.4 Our Fragile Earth: How Close Are We to Climate Catastrophe? by Mark Fischetti (September 26, 2023); 6.1 South Asian Threat? Local Nuclear War = Global Suffering by Alan Robock & Owen Brian Toon (January 1, 2010); 6.2 What Radioactive Fallout Tells Us about Our Nuclear Future by Duy Linh Tu, Nina Berman, Sebastian Tuinder, Dominic Smith, Joseph Polidoro & Jeffery DelViscio (November 14, 2023); 7.1 Will Pluto Be the Last Habitable World? by Caleb A. Scharf (September 28, 2018); 7.2 Can Lucky Planets Get a Second Chance at Life? by Conor Feehly (October 5, 2023); 7.3 Planets Orbiting Dead Stars Foretell the Solar System's Far-Future Fate by Phil Plait (February 9, 2024).

Each author biography was accurate at the time the article was originally published.

INDEX